CW01064517

The Plants of Middle-earth:

Botany and Sub-creation

THE PLANTS OF MIDDLE-EARTH

BOTANY AND

SUB-CREATION

Dinah Hazell

The Kent State University Press
Kent, Ohio

© 2006 by The Kent State University Press, Kent, Ohio 44242
ALL RIGHTS RESERVED
Library of Congress Catalog Card Number 2006011514
ISBN-13: 978-0-87338-883-2
ISBN-10: 0-87338-883-6
Manufactured in China

10 09 08 07 06   5 4 3 2 1

LIBRARY OF CONGRESS CATALOGING-IN-PUBLICATION DATA
Hazell, Dinah, 1942–
The Plants of Middle-earth : botany and sub-creation / Dinah Hazell.
       p.   cm.
Includes bibliographical references and index.
ISBN-13: 978-0-87338-883-2 (hardcover : alk. paper) ∞
ISBN-10: 0-87338-883-6 (hardcover : alk. paper) ∞
1. Tolkien, J. R. R. (John Ronald Reuel), 1892–1973. Lord of the rings.
2. Fantasy fiction, English—History and criticism.
3. Middle Earth (Imaginary place)
4. Plants in literature.
I. Title.
PR6039.032L63388 2006
823'.912—dc22   2006011514

British Library Cataloging-in-Publication data are available.

For George

CONTENTS

PREFACE

Tolkien's Middle-earth is inhabited by many unfamiliar creatures and peoples, among them Dwarves, Elves, Orcs, Ents, and, not least, Half-lings. Each reader forms a personal vision of these characters, and artistic efforts (even Tolkien's) to capture them cannot meet all imaginations. Yet Middle-earth feels very real to its armchair travelers, and one of the main reasons for this familiarity is Tolkien's landscape. Once you have passed through the forests of Ithilien, gasped at the beauty of the *mallorn* in Lothlórien, and smelled the homely grass and blooms of the Shire, you can never again pass through wood, glade, or garden without thinking of Middle-earth and suspecting (or perhaps wishing) that Elves may be near. Tolkien's plant world is the bridge between Bilbo's garden and ours; unlike the fantastic warg or balrog, nasturtiums and oaks are easily visualized.

Tolkien the medievalist and philologist based his Elvish and other languages on those he knew, such as Anglo-Saxon, Middle English, Old Norse, Welsh, Finnish, Latin, and Greek. Curious readers who explore Tolkien's scholarly world may discover that the name of the lofty wooden platform, *flet,* is Middle English for "floor," that the derivation of *mathom* is Old English "máðum," meaning "treasure" or "gift," and that names like Thorin Oakenshield, Durin, and Gandalf are found in the Icelandic saga the *Elder Edda.* Similarly, his botany derives from familiar surroundings. Despite his magical plants like *athelas* and *elanor,* most Middle-earth flora comes from Tolkien's England.

Middle-earth—itself a Middle English appellation, *middelerd,* and Anglo-Saxon *Middangeard*—is at core medieval, and in *The Lord of the Rings* Tolkien preserves and transmits English cultural expression and value, still resonant and relevant to moderns. Readers are usually so absorbed in the tale that they are unaware that their travel through

Middle-earth is also a journey through a repository of centuries-old oral and written tradition. Tolkien drew together the threads of myth, folklore, imagery, and motifs on which English-speaking culture is built and wove them into a great epic for our time, and his botanical life plays a substantial part in that creation. Many of Middle-earth's plants evoke beliefs of powers and qualities found in flora, and Tolkien's landscapes have a character of their own, integral to plot and literary construction. A gardener and plant lover, Tolkien drew on traditional lore to enrich the history of his created world. Yet the plants still grace the modern world, appreciated for their beauty and restorative virtues; we can enter part of Tolkien's imaginative vision in our own yards. My California "English" garden's structured herbaceous borders, tangled cottage beds, fragrant herb garden, and withy fence host many of the plants found in Middle-earth.

This project is the product of thirty years of reading and loving *The Hobbit* and *The Lord of the Rings* and combines my two main passions: medieval English literature and culture, and gardens. My intent in writing this book is to create an environment that will enhance the reader's perspective during future journeys along the roads and through the forests of Middle-earth, and to provide a place for reviving the memory of those trips.

INTRODUCTION

Rather than inventing an alien world into which human and familiar characters are introduced, as in science fiction, Tolkien created a natural environment that is also home to "supernatural" beings and elements, as in medieval works like *Beowulf*. The Shire is always the touchstone to which the hobbits return mentally and against which they (and we) measure the rest of Middle-earth. By creating a sense of familiarity and belonging early and then in each of the cultures encountered, we can meet "others" without feeling estranged. Verisimilitude is maintained even in foreign lands like Mordor.

How does one go about creating an Other World? For Tolkien, it began with a lifelong fascination with language, real and invented. But once there is a language, there must be people to speak the language, a society to support the people, and a world in which the people live. The physical, cultural, and ideological components necessary for believability are all found in Middle-earth. Most folks, whether Men, Hobbits, Dwarves, or Elves, need the basics of clothing, housing, food, possessions, and other facets of material life. And a land needs topography, geography, and flora and fauna, while overall are astronomy and other life sciences, time and space, cosmogony, and technology. Each of the peoples of Middle-earth has its own language, history, traditions, customs, cultural values, social and familial relationships, governance, and economic, legal, and political systems. The world of *The Lord of the Rings* is ethnically diverse, yet there is a shared system by which behavior and character are judged, much of which derives from medieval, yet universal, concepts of human experience.

Tolkien's Middle-earth, like our world, is built upon a double vision of reality, which involves an existential surface and a deeper, mythic level. The two are interactive and symbiotic, bringing substantiality to

· I ·

each other. Much has been said of Tolkien's theory of "primary" and "secondary" worlds and "sub-creation," which he considered an aspect of mythology. The primary world is that of the author's real world, and the secondary that of his (sub)creation. The writer of fantasy, the sub-creator, "hopes that he is drawing on reality" and that "the peculiar quality of this secondary world (if not all the details) are derived from Reality or flowing into it."[1] This structure is mirrored in Middle-earth, where the hobbits' primary world of comfort and adventure is undergirded by a secondary world of myth and lore. History, both temporal and cultural, is central to actual and imagined reality, and Tolkien used elements from his own English and created worlds to achieve a rich mixture of experience and meaning.

Historical depth in *The Lord of the Rings* is achieved through immediacy and association. Beyond the sensory level, there is a stream of cultural connotations and remnants; although readers may not know the details, they are intuitively aware of a subterranean fullness. A good example is Tolkien's use of proverbs (there are at least thirty-seven throughout *The Lord of the Rings*). Many are familiar to us, but some are unique to Middle-earth, and both are often revelatory about the speaker's character. Proverbs draw on cultural associations from our world, while creating a sense of history and wisdom in and for Middle-earth.

Perhaps the best, most palpable example is Tolkien's botany. Like languages and drawing, his education and interest in botany began in childhood under his mother's tutelage and continued throughout his life. He was well acquainted with plant history and cultivation from readings and visits to exhibition gardens, and he enjoyed botanical illustrations. He was especially interested in the development of species, their kinship, and the historical depth their descent evoked.[2] Though his interests encompassed flora from many countries, he drew on plants from his own surroundings, familiar to most readers and experienced through delight in beauty and aroma. His familiarity with botany was more than academic; through his letters we see him weeding, mowing, banding apple trees, hacking old brambles in the December frost, working in the midday heat, watching bullfinches on his sowthistle, and communing with daisies.[3] Tolkien also knew herb lore, which he frequently related to friends during countryside walks, such as the belief that no venomous beast would come within the aroma of common wood avens, which he identified as *Herba Benedicta* (Herb Bennet or the Blessed Plant), and when put in a house it would protect against the devil.[4] Although we may not be steeped in the same lore, we are aware that there are traditional properties to plants and feel significance beneath their surface appearance. In Middle-earth, that awareness is more immediate; most folk acknowledge the history, power, and personality of plants, and some master ancient healing skills, drawing the associative world into the existential. Throughout our study, the tracing of familiar plants' history and lore that underlie their aura and significance replicates the creation of the fictive history and lore that provides cultural and mythic depth to Middle-earth.[5]

In addition, Tolkien's botany serves narrative function, provides sense of place, and enlivens characterization. A look at the flowers, herbs, trees, and other flora of Middle-earth and their stories evokes a fuller and richer appreciation of Tolkien's art and brings us into a more intimate relationship with that imaginary, yet so real, world. To gain this sight, we will be taking a tour of Middle-earth, from Shire to Mordor and back. Before starting, however, we should map out our route and goals. There are many fine works of interpretive literary criticism that provide valuable insights into *The Lord of the Rings*. As in those studies, the project here is to open the text to deeper exploration, but using a different methodology: by attempting to enter Tolkien's personal imaginative world. Using primarily his letters and biographical information, we will try to envision what he saw and what had meaning for him. With botany as a guide, we will investigate other elements of *The Lord of the Rings*, including social and cultural relationships and values, many of which come from materials used by Tolkien in his scholarly work and for his personal pleasure.

Tolkien's plot, themes, motifs, and characters are so engrossing that they can overpower visual imagery; the seemingly familiar can slip into the background, often unnoticed in the presence of the unfamiliar that demands imaginative construction. But it is clear from his meticulous detail to colors, textures, shapes, and other elements that Tolkien intended to create a sensory environment as real to his readers as it was to him. Botany is an excellent starting point for refreshing that experience, and one of the purposes of this book is to evoke impressions of plant life through narrative and visual description. Each chapter is illustrated in a style appropriate to its content, from brilliant watercolors of floral hobbit names, to line drawings reminiscent of medieval herbals, to delicate full-color woodland and garden scenes. And, of course, the grace and strength of trees. The artists were chosen for their love of nature and botany and a sincerity of style that recalls Tolkien's own approach to art.

Hopefully, by the end of our tour, we will be submerged in the primary and secondary worlds of Middle-earth from a different, enriched perspective and see how something as seemingly simple as a bloom can point to the inner life of a literary text. To increase our awareness of the presence of plant life in *The Lord of the Rings* and how such a focus can lead to analysis of wider themes, we begin in the Shire with a look at the floral names of hobbit women. Next we take a botanical tour of Middle-earth, and through our observations we develop a sense of flora's narrative function as it creates verisimilitude and atmosphere, enabling reader participation in characters' experiences and encouraging the examination of overarching concepts like fate and free will. The woodland of Ithilien earns its own chapter for its profusion of exquisite plant life, its contribution to the demonstration of the impact of environment on characters and readers, and as a location that compels exploration of aspects of interpersonal relationships, particularly trust. We then move to the subject of trees, which were central to Tolkien's imagination as witnessed in their transformation into characters, imagery, and symbolism. Through the study of trees in Middle-earth, we learn about the power of nature and its nemesis, modern technology. Finally we end where we began, in the Shire, which is much changed, but as elsewhere in Middle-earth, its restoration involves plant life and teaches us the different ways and meanings of recovery.

CHAPTER I

HOBBIT NAMES

he botanical names that abound in hobbit culture give life and color to their namesakes and reflect the close association between folk and flower. Nearly all of Tolkien's characters (except Men) are unusual or fantastic, and all but hobbits have names created outside of the ordinary to suit their nature. There are a few exceptions: several families of Men bear botanical surnames like Ferny, Goatleaf, Heathertoes, Appledore, Thistlewood, and Rushlight. All are from Bree, the singular community where Men and hobbits dwell together. The most memorable Bree-man's name is Barliman Butterbur. Although still used as an herbal remedy, butterbur may not be familiar to most modern readers, but it was well known to medieval herbalists, particularly as a cure for pestilential fevers; in Germany it is still called *Pestilenzwurz*. Its large, broad, round leaves were used for wrapping butter, hence its name. It's likely that Tolkien chose the name for its sound, as Barliman Butterbur does roll smoothly off the tongue, and its plump namesake is certainly never at a loss for words.

When the four hobbit travelers from the Shire meet some of the Bree-folk at The Prancing Pony, they find the botanical names "odd,"[1] apparently forgetting that many Shire women bear floral names. Hobbits find their own names more "natural," usually related to their living environment, like Burrows and Longholes; some are even more earthy, like Maggot and Grubb. Other popular sources of hobbit names are occupations (as in medieval times), like Roper, Butcher, Sandyman, Greenhand, and Hayward, and physical attributes (real or imagined) like Proudfoot and Goodbody, while a few have plant names, like Mugwort and Cotton. Botanical names are steeped in associations and lore; for example, mugwort (*Artemesia vulgaris*) was famed in medieval times for its medicinal and magical properties. *Mucgwyrt,* the "oldest of plants" and "Mother of Herbs"[2] protected homes from evil and eased travel weariness, as well as cured illnesses with remedies contained in herbals like the Old English *Herbarium* and the Anglo-Saxon *Lacnunga*.[3]

The Cotton and Gamgee families are closely related in name as well as through friendship and marriage. Although in hobbit history the latter name is derived from the village Gamwich, it actually comes from Gamgee tissue, the name for cotton wool used in Birmingham when

Tolkien was young. Gaffer Gamgee was inspired by an odd local character to whom Tolkien gave the alliterated name for comic effect to amuse his children.[4]

Hobbits are mostly unknown to the rest of Middle-earth, remembered vaguely in myth and needing to be added to Treebeard's old lists of the lore of Living Creatures. But after being introduced to hobbits, we become accustomed to them quite quickly, overlooking their hairy feet and diminutive size, thanks to their "Englishness": bright vests, love of food and beer, pipe smoking, and, of course, gardening. Tolkien gave many halflings ordinary names that are easily remembered and visualized, reinforcing the familiarity of the Shire and its inhabitants so that they are always central to the reader.

Before looking at individual hobbit names, a brief discussion of the word *hobbit* is irresistible. Tolkien claims that it appeared one day unbidden and that there was no linguistic origin for it, although he invented an etymology from Old English (*hol:* "hole"; *bytla:* "dweller"); like several other words derived from that language, *holbytla* is appropriately preserved in Rohan language, which is based on Anglo-Saxon. In Letter 319 Tolkien considers the possibility that *hobbit* might have come from an unconscious childhood memory of characters in a story (one of several theories offered by readers) but thinks it unlikely.[5] However, it is tempting to imagine that the word was buried in his memory, a bit of the "leaf-mould" that occasionally surfaces,[6] and we may look to Middle English literature for clues. The words *hob* and *hobbis* appear in several fourteenth-century works, like *The Mum and the Sothsegger* and *Richard the Redeless,* which are approximately contemporary with the *Gawain*-poet's works Tolkien translated. Not all definitions of *hob* and *hobbis* glossed by scholars apply here, but several seem quite relevant: a rustic, one of common class, a country clown. While hardly capturing the full hobbit nature, these descriptions hint at the kernel of the mysteriously appearing name for rural beings who can be "comic" and "laughable," especially Sam's "comicness, peasantry" and "Englishry."[7]

Most botanical hobbit names are women's given names, like Poppy, Daisy, and Primula. The Entish reluctance to divulge one's true name reflects the universal belief that names hold the essence of a person's nature and once revealed can confer power over the owner. Conversely, attributes can be bestowed through name giving, and floral names be-

What's in a Name?

While Tolkien often chose words for their sound, a close look at many of them suggests that meaning had more influence than might be suspected or claimed. For example, names he gave to his dwarves from the *Elder Edda,* when translated from the Old Norse, fit their owners' characteristics quite well. Thrain is translated as Yearner, descriptive of a dwarf who is restless and greedy for gold; Gloin (ON Gleamer) is chief fire-maker, with his brother, of the dwarves; Thror (Thrive) is head of the dwarf dynasty; Thorin (Darer) leads the dwarves into battle; Durin (Doorward) holds the secret to entering Moria; and Bombur (Tubby) needs no explanation.[8]

queath not only loveliness but also virtues associated with the bloom or plant. Perhaps a flower name was chosen for a hobbit maid-child because it brought back some memory, like Aragorn's thoughts of Arwen as he gazed on a golden *elanor* blossom in Lothlórien,[9] or maybe just because it was a favorite.

It's obvious that Tolkien, like Bilbo, loved flowers, and it seems he wished to portray the spirit of Shire women through that sweet, occasionally thorny, timeless imagery. A bouquet could be gathered from hobbit female names, or they might decorate a medieval illumination like those in the manuscripts Tolkien studied. Now, we will look at some of the flowers for which hobbit women are named. Although we don't know many of the characters well, we can imagine what parents hoped for in their daughters, and, with characters we do know, whether they grew into their names. And even if given (by hobbit parents or Tolkien) without deliberate purpose, a name is still evocative. The two hobbit women we know best are Lobelia Sackville-Baggins and Rosie Cotton, so we'll start with them.

Lobelia Sackville-Baggins

Lobelia is one of the few flowers used by Tolkien that does not have a lengthy history. Introduced in the eighteenth century from Africa and the Americas, it was not cultivated extensively in England until the nineteenth century. There are over two hundred varieties of lobelia, annual and perennial, wild and cultivated, ranging from small clumping and trailing plants that reseed themselves throughout the garden (often in unwanted places like between bricks in pathways), to sturdy spiking stalks, all in vivid colors. The upright varieties, such as *Lobelia cardinalis,* sleep over the winter but reemerge each spring in readiness for bright summer bloom. Lobelia's last name is reminiscent of Vita Sackville-West, designer of the great garden at Sissinghurst Castle planted from 1930 onward, and might be a tribute to her, or perhaps it's a satirical poke at Lobelia's visions of grandeur.

Rosie Cotton

Unlike the newcomer lobelia, the rose, which grew in abundance in Tolkien's garden,[10] is laden with history and symbolism. Roses have been prized since at least Roman times and developed over the ensuing centuries, but many of the roses we now see are "modern" roses, developed in the last two centuries. For many of us, the best rose is the "old" rose. And the most ancient cultivated old roses are the Gallicas, perhaps introduced to Britain by the Romans and known to the Anglo-Saxons, with many varieties today. The *R. Gallica officinalis,* also called the apothecary's rose for its medicinal uses, is probably the oldest of the Gallicas. It is the red rose of the Lancasters, as opposed to the white *Rosa alba* of the Yorks. Another old rose family is the heavily scented Damask, which tradition holds was brought to England by returning Crusaders.

There are two roses native to Britain that are easily envisioned in Middle-earth. One is the *Rosa canina* (briar, dog rose, wild rose), which was one of William Morris's favorites and appeared in his garden, designs, and verse. It grows to around ten feet and can be cultivated as a dense shrub or on trellises. Although it has waned in popularity as more showy roses have taken prominence and is now used as root stock for hybridizing, it still graces the English countryside in hedgerows.

The other is the sweet briar, *Rosa eglanteria*. Like the *Rosa canina*, it can climb up trellises and through hedges. It has a decidedly "Took-ish" nature, like the family famous for its adventurousness (the usu-ally complacent Bilbo was spurred on by his Tookish side).[11] One of the most treasured wild plants in England, it is loved for its apple-like scent, predominant in its leaves; due to its aroma and piercing thorns, the sweet briar represents pleasure and pain. Eglantine Took, Pippin's mother, is not the only namesake of this flower; readers of Chaucer will recognize one of his most controversial characters, Eglantine the Prior-ess. Scholars debate over this choice of name; one widespread theory is that it is taken from medieval romance heroines and thus inappropriate for a clergywoman, and other suggestions include association with a historic person or the flower and possible Christian connotations.

The rose has wide, sometimes conflicting symbolism. It represents love and secrecy, transient love, change and mutability, steadfastness, religious devotion, and purity. Along with the lily, it is dedicated to the Virgin Mary, and the rosary takes its name from the compressed petals that once formed the beads.

Despite its delicate beauty and reputation for touchiness, the rose is remarkably hardy. Many will thrive with little or no care, and an unwanted plant can be very difficult to retire; once firmly rooted, it will persevere. While there are countless roses, they escape commonality and are treasured, as is Rosie Cotton by Sam, who comforts himself during hardship with thoughts of her and her brothers in happier days.[12]

Daisy Gamgee and Daisy Boffin

Tolkien's career as an artist was as long, and nearly as productive, as his literary. He did few naturalistic floral illustrations; rather, flowers appear as design elements in heraldic devices and floral alphabets. But his early work, drawn from his surroundings, featured landscapes, buildings, and trees, a focus maintained in the details of *The Lord of the Rings.* Like William Morris, whose literary technique and themes were among Tolkien's inspirations and with whom he shared a love of medievalism, a disdain for modern technology and industrialization, the desire to protect forest and trees, and a preference for homely craft, Tolkien chose flowers that graced the fields and woods in which he spent his youth and treasured throughout his life. One such is the daisy, a favorite motif of Morris's designs. Morris was also a famous gardener, influential in the cottage style developed in the late nineteenth century based on free-flowing, traditional native plantings rather than rigid compositions of ornamental hybrids and exotics.

There are many varieties of daisies, so the image will vary depending on the reader's locale and environment. But let's concentrate on one used by Morris, with the thought that it might also be the bloom envisioned for Middle-earth: the *Bellis perennis* or English daisy, a miniature white bloom tinged with pink, found in lawns. Today, there are two dozen forms of *Bellis perennis*, many of which were cultivated by the eighteenth century; Elizabethan gardeners collected double forms and the "hen and chickens" in which small blossoms ring the main flower,[13] with which Tolkien was familiar. In Letter 312, Tolkien tells of some red daisies in his border garden that reseeded into the grass, where they became lawn daisies and struggled for life. A few seeds reached rich soil and produced a plant with an enormous bloom, which he admired but compared (within its hearing) to *Bellis perennis* and found no improvement on the original. In response, overnight a number of delicate pink-tipped blossoms emerged from the flower, which Tolkien likened to "little elvish daisies" with the charm of "an airy crown."[14]

Marigold Cotton

As in botany, hobbit familial relationships are quite complex. For example, Sam Gamgee's sister, Marigold, married Tom Cotton, Rosie Cotton's brother, and thus was also Sam's sister-in-law. (Even Tolkien got confused, referring to Frodo initially as Bilbo's cousin, then nephew.[15]) At a simpler level, the marigold is a relative of the daisy. The plant is self-seeding and thrives in poor soil even when neglected. It was, and is, a staple in cottage gardens. However, it is not the tufty-bedding *Tagetes* (French or African marigold) popular in England and America since the early twentieth century, but the pot marigold (*Calendula officinalis*)[16] that was ubiquitous in medieval kitchen gardens, where flowers, herbs, and greens like *wortes* were raised for utility and as part of an often-meager diet.[17] The blossoms were used to relieve wasp and bee stings, and the bright orange petals produced a light yellow dye and added spice to salads and pottages. In the seventeenth century, Culpeper recommended the plant in his *Complete Herbal and English Physician* for strengthening the heart and treating smallpox and measles, among other afflictions.[18] The pot marigold symbolized enduring love.

Pansy Bolger

As modest as the marigold and equally beloved is the pansy. We see them in many sizes and hues, but the *Viola tricolor,* heartsease, is the

traditional form, native to England. Its bloom is marked in the center with bright yellow to attract bumblebees and other insects to its nectar. Considered beautiful by Morris, it still grows wild, along with bluebells, forget-me-nots, and primroses, between the trees in the orchard of his Red House.[19] Heartsease was also grown in medieval gardens, as seen in tapestries, and was known in Elizabethan times. The ancestor of modern violas (or pansies as they are often called), heartsease (or Johnny Jump-up) was crossbred in the early nineteenth century, and the hybrids produced were named "pansy." "Violas" followed in 1860, then "violettas," both of which have stayed in cultivation longer than the native heartsease.[20]

The name "Heartsease" has multiple associations. Healing properties were ascribed to the plant, some of which have been confirmed by modern science; it was believed to stimulate the immune system, cleanse the blood, and treat skin complaints. Culpeper lists convulsions in children, falling sickness, pleurisy, and other ailments among those cured by a decoction of the herb and flower.[21] Its "Two Faces in a Hood" seemed to be kissing, thus easing the heart. Like many other blooms in Middle-earth, it represented love and remembrance, but it was also associated with wantonness, hence the name "Love in Idleness" and its use as a love potion. In *A Midsummer Night's Dream,* it is the herb used by Oberon to enchant Titania as she sleeps in a grove amidst oxlips, wild thyme, violets, musk roses, and eglantine:

The juice of it on sleeping eyelids laid
Will make or man or woman madly dote
Upon the next live creature that it sees. (II.i.170–72)

Primula Baggins (née Brandybuck)

The oxlips in Titania's bed are *Primula elatior,* a rare British native. More common is the *Primula vulgaris,* the English primrose that has graced woodlands and gardens for several centuries. "Primrose" derives from Latin for "first rose," since it is one of the earliest blooming flowers in spring; the light yellow *vulgaris* is thus one of the earliest to produce nectar, while the hybrids, often in showy, bright colors with enlarged petals and leaves, do not. It was believed to be a protection against evil and, like heartsease, was used as a love potion; it also found

its way into medicinal cures, potpourris, cosmetics, and kitchen dishes. Folklore tells us that children eating the flowers could see fairies. Bringing thirteen or more primrose blooms into the house was considered good luck, while a single flower would bring misfortune.[22] Primula Baggins, Frodo's mother, certainly had an unhappy fate, drowning with her husband on the Brandywine and leaving Frodo an orphan.

Poppy Bolger

Poppy Bolger is Bilbo's second cousin and is also related through marriage via the Chubbs to the Old Took, but we know her only from the genealogy charts. If she lived up to her name, she would be a vibrant, versatile character of long lineage. Poppies are ancient; seeds have been found in Egyptian tombs, and the plants have splashed across cornfields and served multitudinous purposes ever since. There are many varieties of poppies, from tiny to stately, in annual, biennial, and perennial forms. They are self-perpetuating, reseeding themselves freely, and grow both wild and in the garden. Poppy blooms are stunning but short-lived; silky petals, buds, and heads of the blossom sit atop slender, graceful stalks surrounded by lacelike foliage.

Most hark back to the British native *Papaver rhoeas,* which still can be seen in breathtaking brilliant drifts in farmlands and has previously traveled to the continent and been developed into forms such as the Dutch poppy. The bright red bloom symbolizes remembrance of the blood shed by dead warriors; the plant also signifies fertility and serves as an antidote for those bewitched in love. This wild poppy, also known as the corn or field poppy, has legions of uses. For centuries, no part of the plant has gone ignored; root, seed, flower, head, juice, and whole plant are prepared into syrup, tincture, oil, distilled water, decoction, and poultice forms, and combined in healing compounds. Medicinal applications are almost countless, the flowers color wine, the seeds and oil are used in baking and cooking, and cosmetic uses include hair dye.

There is another poppy that is equally dramatic but of shady reputation: the *Papaver somniferum,* the opium poppy. It's an outstanding annual ornamental plant, growing two to three feet with single and double flower varieties in many colors, and is more common than many other varieties of poppy for cottage gardening. It is also the source of opium and its derivatives, which come from the juice of the unripe heads. The calming properties of this poppy have been known for centuries, and so have its narcotic and adverse effects. In ancient times, its use as a sleep aid gave it the name "Poppies of the Lethe" after the river of forgetfulness.[23] Nevertheless, it's a stunner in the flowerbed and deserves its popularity, but even when its history is put out of mind and the plant is enjoyed strictly for its beauty, an aura of mystery surrounds it, reminding us of the way in which cultural and historical associations may cling beyond conscious thought.

Compared to most of the flowers we've seen so far, the lily may seem too ornamental or lofty for the cottage garden. Nevertheless, it's still a favorite, especially the Madonna lily (*Lilium candidum*), which may have been introduced to Britain by the Romans; it was used to treat wounds and grew where there had been encampment sites. It was known to Bede, who associated it with the Virgin for its white petals and golden anthers, which represented physical purity and a radiant soul.[24] Lilies had pride of place in medieval enclosed gardens and as church decoration, especially in Lady Chapels, and, with roses, are associated with the Virgin and nearly ubiquitous in medieval and Renaissance Marian iconography.

There are many other popular garden lilies in a rather confusing array. The Crown Imperial (not a true lily but the *Fritillaria imperialis*) is a majestic, symmetrical plant long seen in paintings and embroideries. The Turk's cap lily (*L. martagon*) is considered native to the British Isles, perhaps the only lily to claim that origin rather than importation. It was known in Britain by Elizabethan times; there were five forms in the seventeenth century and over twenty in the early nineteenth, although its popularity waned to three forms by the end of the century due to the arrival of the tiger lily and other varieties from Asia.[25] The tiger lily became a fast favorite and appeared in the old-fashioned garden of Tennyson's "Song," although seen sadly at the end of the season when

> Heavily hangs the broad sunflower
>> Over its grave i' the earth so chilly;
> Heavily hangs the hollyhock,
>> Heavily hangs the tiger-lily.

Perhaps more at home in Middle-earth is the lily of the valley (*Convallaria majalis*), a woodland plant that prefers the company of other plants to cultivation. Still, it is popular and considered lucky in the garden, although unlucky when brought into the house. The delicate plant with its snowdrop blossoms has been imagined as a ladder for fairies. It is also known as "Our Lady's Tears" from the legend that it sprang up at the foot of the Cross where tears were shed.[26] Sussex folklore tells that heaven granted that the plants would grow wild where the blood of St. Leonard fell during his battle with a dragon.[27] It has been cultivated since medieval times with aromatic, culinary, and medicinal uses; even in the earlier twentieth century there was a folk remedy for treating cuts and abrasions by covering them with a fresh lily of the valley leaf. Whether the relatively modest lily of the valley or one of the more magnificent varieties may be what Tolkien had in mind for Rosie Cotton's mother, any form of lily would impart a quiet dignity to its namesake.

Belladonna Baggins (née Took)

Lilies lead us, by a somewhat circuitous route, to Bilbo's mother, Belladonna, to whom we are introduced in *The Hobbit*. Her father, the Old Took, was head of the clan, which was noted for its somewhat peculiar nature and rumored to have had a fairy wife in its ancestry. They were also rich, and Belladonna's father built luxurious Bag End for her and her husband, Bungo Baggins.[28] The belladonna lily may be an apt flower for which to name so remarkable a woman, both in meaning, "fair lady," perhaps derived from the use of its juice to make eyes brilliant by dilating the pupils, and appearance. It is not really a lily, but the *Amaryllis belladonna;* the bulbous plant was imported from the Cape of Good Hope and popular in the mid-nineteenth and early twentieth centuries. Dormant in the winter, it produces leaves in the spring that die back before the silvery pink, somewhat eerily naked blooms appear in summer on stout stalks.

However, the story becomes stranger, as the *Amaryllis* may not be the first plant that comes to mind when one hears the name belladonna. Rather, it may be the deadly nightshade (*Atropa belladonna*), a European plant known for centuries and notorious for its poisonous properties. Although used medicinally into modern times, it lives in legend as the killer of children who eat the berries and as the cause of madness. The invasion of Scotland in the eleventh century by Sweyn, the Danish king of England, is said to have been repelled by drugging the invading army with deadly nightshade and killing the soldiers in their sleep.[29] Considering Belladonna Baggins's position and nature (having given up adventures after her marriage), perhaps we should assume that it is the belladonna lily, not the deadly nightshade, that Tolkien had in mind when naming her. Still, it is a curious choice.

Camellia Baggins (née Sackville)

The camellia may be the only hothouse flower in our Shire bouquet. The camellia was one of the Chinese imports that arrived in Europe and Britain in the nineteenth century, an influx that excited gardeners. A shrubby plant with delicate blooms in the white, pink, and red ranges, it is somewhat touchy and needs to be sheltered from wind; the plant does not grow successfully in all parts of England. Camellia seems a rather exotic name for a hobbit, though we don't know its namesake well enough to judge its aptness.

But Camellia Baggins is of interest as a demonstration of the complicated social customs and genealogies Tolkien created for hobbits. Compound last names are unusual among the hobbits we know, and the derivation of Sackville-Baggins can be traced to Camellia, Otho's mother and Lobelia's mother-in-law. If the head of a family died without a male heir, the title could be passed to the eldest grandson through the daughter. This occurred with Otho, who, according to custom, took his mother's family name, Sackville, as a sign of the courtesy headship of the family and opted to retain his father's name (last), thus Sackville-Baggins.[30]

Peony Burrows

Like the camellia, the peony has a sophisticated look that might seem out of place in the old-fashioned flora we're envisioning for Middle-earth. However, peonies are said to be the oldest of cultivated flowers and grew in Anglo-Saxon gardens. The date of the introduction of the *Paeonia officinalis* (red apothecary peony) from its native southern Europe is unknown, but the *P. mascula* may have come across the Channel to the island of Steep Holm with Augustinians in the late twelfth and early thirteenth centuries, where it is said to be the only place it grew (and still grows) wild in the British Isles,[31] and more forms arrived in the mid-sixteenth century. In medieval times, the seeds were used for a peppery spice and, when drunk in wine or mead, brought sleep and freedom from nightmares.

The bush yields crimson, pink, purple, or white blossoms, but not easily; it may take years to bloom. A tree version, the moutan, was introduced from China and Siberia in the nineteenth century and was widely

developed, with three hundred single and double forms appearing by the end of the century.[32] This coincided with the nostalgic creation of old-fashioned gardens that demanded improved plant forms of favorites like the peony, delphinium, and sweet pea, and the recovery of lost or forgotten plants from cottage gardens like old roses.[33] And this was the time of the movement toward simplicity in home and garden, reminiscent of preindustrial times and medieval culture valued by Tolkien. Like many then and now, he treasured the beauty of a "flowery plot" such as the grassy bed on which the fourteenth-century *Pearl*-poet's Dreamer is lulled to sleep, cushioned by "gilofre, gyngure, and gromylyoun /

And pyonys powdered ay betwene" ("gillyflower, ginger, and gromwell crowned, / And peonies powdered all between"; I:43–44).[34]

And Others

There are many other hobbits with botanical names. For example, Mentha Brandybuck, Angelica Baggins, and Gilly Baggins, named for the gillyflower, the clove-pink dianthus (the name also applied to stock and wallflower), are named for plants valued for their flavor and sweet aroma. The gillyflower added not only fragrance to an Elizabethan nosegay but, like many flowers, also had symbolic meaning:

> Gillyflowers is for gentleness,
> Which in me shall remain,
> Hoping that no sedition shall
> Depart our hearts in twain.
> As soon the sun shall lose his course,
> The moon against her kind
> Shall have no light, if that I do
> Once put you from my mind.[35]

Other flower namesakes include Celandine Brandybuck, Pimpernel Took, Asphodel Burrows, and Amaranth Brandybuck, while Salvia Bolger and Myrtle Burrows bear the names of herbs and shrubs. Tree names include Rowan Gammidge, Sam's great-grandmother, and Filibert Bolger, one of the few males with a botanical given name. As we will see during our tour, many of these plants are found growing in Middle-earth.

Since we've been looking at hobbit women and their names, this is a good time to sneak in a word about women in *The Lord of the Rings*. They are often variously seen as idealized, stereotypical, passive, one-dimensional, and lacking in attributes valued in the twentieth century, which may be less than fair. Like other elements in *The Lord of the Rings*, Tolkien's characterization of women has roots in earlier cultures and literature, such as the Old Norse and Anglo-Saxon valkyrie and warrior-queen/noblewoman, who were often subordinate to the narra-

tive but had significant function, and medieval romance heroines, who embodied moral values and were frequently assertive actors despite the damsel-in-distress topos. These models can be seen in Tolkien's women, sometimes in combination, like Éowyn, who moves from shield-maiden of Rohan warrior society to the courtly world of Gondor. Galadriel may be seen as Eddic light elf, associated with magic wells, spinning and weaving, gift giving, and swan-maidens; as a valkyrie who passes the fare-well cup; as an Anglo-Saxon noblewoman of generous nature, imposing stature, dignity, and eloquence, wisdom and prophecy; and as a courtly queen of elevated speech, manner and custom.[36] Goldberry, although a folkloric water sprite figure, is warm, welcoming, and personable. Here, as elsewhere, Tolkien enlivens traditional images and imbues them with individuality.

Many of Tolkien's women wield great power, and even lesser characters than Galadriel and Éowyn have strength, though of a less superhuman kind. Although hobbit society seems patriarchal, Tolkien describes it as "patrilinear": family names pass through the male line, and the eldest male is the titular head of the family, but only after both his father and mother die. As Tolkien explains in Letter 214, hobbit marriages are a dyarchy, so that husband and wife have equal status though different functions, and women continue as titular head of the family after the husband's death, like Laura Baggins, who ruled the family for sixteen years; Lalia the Great; and Bilbo's mother, the fabulous Belladonna Took.[37] Rosie Cotton's spunk in her relationship with Sam lets us know that she will not be a silent partner, and the umbrella-wielding Lobelia Sackville-Baggins is one of the few hobbits (male or female) to defy Sharkey's domination, even though her son was part of the enemy regime, albeit a pawn trapped by his own thirst for power.[38]

While the bouquet of female hobbit names brings us the sweet scent and beauty of the Shire, plant personality and lore also tells us something about its inhabitants. The flowers are valued for their simplicity and, though humble, they have grandeur in their hardiness and lack of pretension. Most of the names are associated with love, remembrance, and fidelity—the components of successful relationships in both marriage and friendship—and with healing. However, like people and hobbits, plants can have both good and bad natures, sometimes mixed, and fulfilling the promise of floral symbolism often requires effort and choice by the namesake. While we are in the Shire, we will begin our tour of Middle-earth, guided by its botany.

CHAPTER 2

FROM SHIRE TO MORDOR

A Botanical Tour of Middle-earth

efore beginning our tour, we need to consider the role of botany in Tolkien's literary creation. It serves many functions; at surface, it draws the eye to natural beauty and gives a sense of place and reality to the surroundings. As we have seen with floral hobbit names, botany also carries a subtle history and imagery that convey a feeling of depth and heritage. Throughout *The Lord of the Rings,* Tolkien describes locales by their topography and flora, which tells us much about their atmosphere and inhabitants. Such environmental evocation also expresses the feelings of the travelers and hints at experiences to be encountered. As we will see, the state of plant life reflects the personality of a place and helps us imagine its soul.

Much of the Fellowship's time is spent traveling, and though they pass through many locations quickly, we still envision the terrain: springy turf underfoot, lines of trees along far-off rivers, rolling gray-green hills in the distance, rocky crags with wizened shrubs. The environment often intensifies action and emotions, like the gloomy land between Weathertop and the road to Rivendell. The wild flora, scanty grass, and tree roots that loom from cliffs overhead create a dark menace that reflects Frodo's pain from the attack on Weathertop and the continuing fear of Black Riders. Relief comes in the sunny trolls' glade, and on the hazel- and heather-covered slopes where the Company meets Glorfindel.

Later, as the Company boats down the Great River, the landscape sets the atmosphere as they begin their journey toward danger. The desolate Brown Lands on the east (once the Entwives' lush gardens) are completely barren and wasted, and the treeless plains of grass and hissing, withering reeds and ferns on the west are a somber contrast to, and grievous reminder of, the beauty and joy of Lórien that has been left behind. As they come nearer to Wilderland, the river banks become rocky and steep, matted with inhospitable thorn and bramble, sharp bitter sloe, and treacherous creeping plants, and the tense, hostile environment presages the impending Orc attack. Farther downriver, approaching the Emyn Muil, the trees that cling to the rocky ravine are described as "thrawn,"[1] a Scottish word meaning "twisted," "misshapen," "perverse," definitions of the English word "thrown" that are now obsolete. The appearance of a word that has absorbed defunct special meaning reminds us of Tolkien's

B<small>RAMBLE</small>

use of archaic syntax and words, like "rede" (advice) that are often from Old and Middle English; this device distances us from modern times and enriches our vision of Middle-earth as a heroic, epic world.[2]

During their travels, Sam and Frodo must scramble through many stone gullies and crevices, with little or no vegetation to cheer or aid them. As they pass through Morgai, they witness the plants' last struggle for life, which is lost in Mordor, and they must battle the cutting, biting brambles and insects that eke out sustenance from the pitiful land. The flora is in torment, its growth stunted and tortured by lack of the natural resources and spirit that are destroyed under the Enemy's influence, which the hobbits must soon face fully as they proceed to Mt. Doom and fight with the same wracked earth and deprivation that marks Sauron's poison.

The final road traveled in *The Lord of the Rings* leads to the Grey Havens, and the last plant named on that journey is the hazel, which grows in thickets on Shire hills along the way. Hazel had protective and magical powers, and its wood was used for sorcerers' wands. As a symbol of fertility, the hazel reflects the bountiful growth of flora and family in the restored Shire, and its association with knowledge and immortality resonates with Elven nature. Whether by chance (if chance it was) or design, Tolkien chose a perfect plant companion for the meeting of rustic hobbits and shimmering Elves on the brink of their worlds.

Our botanical tour of Middle-earth must, of course, start in the Shire, where the four hobbit comrades' adventures begin and end. And the best place is Bilbo's garden, though the visit will be brief; seen through the window of Bag End, snapdragons, sunflowers, and trailing nasturtiums glow in the late afternoon sun. In his letter to Katherine Farrer of August 7, 1954, shortly after *The Fellowship* was published, Tolkien tells of his fight with the editors to retain the spelling "nasturtians" for its unpretentiousness compared to the botanical erudition of "nasturtium."[3] Although he eventually lost the battle, the anecdote expresses his desire to create a homely, earthy environment in the Shire.

This is the only peek we have at Bilbo's flower garden, but we also know that he has a lawn, which Sam cuts with shears, as Tolkien was known to do; he was seen trimming the grass with scissors "closely and evenly" in the garden of a friend with whom he was staying, as well as weeding and tending the beds "meticulously."[4] Historically, although there were specialists, gardeners like Sam were simple laborers in the Middle Ages; but in the Shire, as Frodo explains to Faramir, they are honored. Sam and his father have tended the garden at Bag End for many years, and Sam's vision of the world is centered around his lifelong close relationship with plants and the soil; his rustic simplicity, solidity, and common sense are the foundation of his strength of character, which is revealed as the Quest unfolds. For many, including Tolkien, Sam the gardener is the "chief hero" of *The Lord of the Rings*.[5]

We are given glimpses of the Shire's apple orchards and vineyards, evidenced by their harvests, before Frodo, Sam, Pippin, and Merry leave Hobbiton. As they travel toward Crickhollow, the land comes more fully into view, dotted with woods, grassland, meadows, rivers, villages, hedgerows, dikes, and farms. Turnip fields on the approach to Farmer Maggot's spread (and his mushrooms) remind us that the Shire is an agricultural society, which helps us understand its culture. Life at Farmer Maggot's seems typical, with a large family and workers jostling around the dinner table, at which there is room for unexpected guests. The scene is one of plenty, with the good, homely food that appears frequently during the hobbits' travels. Food in *The Lord of the Rings* carries more than nutritional value; it is the centerpiece of hospitality, friendship, and comfort at Farmer Maggot's, Tom Bombadil's, and elsewhere. Loss of those essential qualities during times of scarcity and hunger in the later stages of the Quest heightens the hobbits' sense of deprivation and isolation.

The next phase of our tour would be the Old Forest and the Withywindle, but we're going to bypass that stop since it will be discussed later. So, we now reach the home of Tom Bombadil and Goldberry, River-daughter. Tom Bombadil (whose name, like his speech, reverberates with poetic meter) is more important than Tolkien realized, who considered him a "comment" rather than a narrative necessity.[6] He misjudged Bombadil's impact on readers, who find Tom fascinating and disagree with the author's opinion that the character needs little philosophizing about. Tolkien does concede that Bombadil is of some importance as a representative of "pure" natural science that seeks knowledge of other beings without the need to utilize the knowledge; Tom is an exemplar of the study of Botany versus the practice of Agriculture.[7] Tom and Goldberry have a unique relationship to nature and plant life; they live in concord with natural forces, and though Tom is "master," he does not try to exercise control or ownership, which Goldberry says would be a "burden."[8] They each tend the environment in their own way but with a single purpose, and they symbolize the antithesis of the modern technology and industrialization that Tolkien demonized in Sauron's power.

Bombadil and Goldberry's relationship with nature is reflected in their home life. Though quite individual in appearance and personality, they nevertheless work and live in complete harmony, even sharing domestic chores. Their house is a joy to visit, a completely safe haven on the edge of danger, filled with warmth and song. It's furnished with natural materials, and both Tom and Goldberry dress in floral hues and ornamentation. Her gold belt is shaped like flag lilies, and her clothing reflects her association with river and rain; even her movements recall the sound of water. She is surrounded by white water lilies, poetic symbol of purity of heart and noted in herb lore for cooling and calming effects, mirroring the atmosphere of their home. As Tom notes, had it not been for his gathering of lilies at season's end, he would not have found and rescued the hobbits. Although their meeting was unplanned but not unexpected, he points to the repeated theme of the relationship of chance to a guiding and directing force, which leads to a major issue that threads throughout the plot: fate, free will, and determinism. Regardless of how the hobbits arrived at Bombadil's house, awakening to the sight of bright red blossoms against shiny pole-bean leaves, a flower garden, and neatly shaved lawn and hedges drives away somber thoughts and, for the moment, fears.

Tom directs the hobbits to Bree and Barliman Butterbur's inn, The Prancing Pony. Once they finally arrive and are joined by Strider, their trip to Rivendell becomes more dangerous, but it is also enriched by the Ranger's store of knowledge, history, and lore. Just before the attack by Black Riders on Weathertop, Strider tells of Beren and Lúthien Tinúviel, the story that Tolkien began very early and that was central to his *Silmarillion* mythology; versions appear in prose in the *Book of Lost Tales* and in verse in *The Lay of Beleriand*. Strider's presentation is one of the most exquisite pieces of poetry in *The Lord of the Rings,* magical in its imagery of music, moonlight and star-shimmer, and Elven-flowers. Through winter and spring, across soft green grass, over hill and wood, and amid hemlock, linden, and beech, Beren pursues and finally captures the Elven maid, who surrenders her immortality with the liaison. The lay that Strider sings and the brief history he relays are but a snippet of their sorrowful tale and perilous adventures, which are told elsewhere in Elven-lore. The story was born in a woodland glade where Edith and Tolkien spent time during the war, while he was at an outpost of the Humber Garrison at Roos in Yorkshire. She was the inspiration for Lúthien in beauty, singing, and dancing, and their relationship was Tolkien's own "personal romance."[9] The love, devotion, and hardships of the mythic couple resonate with Tolkien's marriage; he and Edith were Beren and Lúthien, as reflected by those names on their gravestones.

Returning to the world of Middle-earth and its dangers, we find one of the few plants (and only herb) created by Tolkien: *athelas*. While on Weathertop, Strider's finding and use of *athelas* to ease Frodo's wound introduces the plant as a rare but effective treatment, and the combination of the plant's properties and Aragorn's healing power is typical of the medico-magic of medieval leechcraft (OE *læce,* "healer," "physician"). But Aragorn gives only part of the lore surrounding the ancient

Butterbur
Petasites albus

plant, and we learn later that *athelas* heralds his arrival as king in Minas Tirith. When Aragorn calls for the plant in the Houses of Healing and treats the heroes who have been wounded in battle, the old wives' tale that recalls the rhyme identifying *athelas* as the plant with which the king can dispel the black breath reveals Aragorn's status, and the news of his arrival is soon spread. The name for the herb seems to have its root in Middle English *athel,* noble by birth or character, a chief or lord (like the historical Athelred), and *atheling,* prince. Thus the plant's common name of *kingsfoil* is appropriate.

Healing is also the province of Rivendell, where wounds of body and spirit fade through the arts of the Elves and the magic of the place. Unfortunately, there is little botany there to detain us on our tour, so we must pass through quickly, missing the wonders. There are gardens at Rivendell, where the atmosphere is so pleasant that it seems like summer in autumn, but the plant life is not described. However, the next haven for the travelers, which is now the Fellowship, more than compensates for the lack of floral detail at Rivendell. But before reaching Lothlórien, they pass through inhospitable country and deadly danger, and when they leave the vale of Rivendell the terrain becomes rough and barren. Before being repelled by Carahdras and heading toward Moria, the travelers have a brief respite in Hollin, the ancient Elven-home Eregion.

Eregion was founded in the Elder Days near Moria by Noldor Elven-smiths who sought *mithril.* They were close friends with Durin's folk, and a road led from Hollin to the gates of Moria, marked at the end by two huge holly trees that still stand when the Fellowship reaches the gate. The Elves, aided by Sauron, crafted the three Elven rings of power, but when they discovered that Sauron had fashioned the One Ring, war ensued; both Elves and Dwarves were defeated, and an antipathy arose between the two, which makes the friendship between Legolas and Gimli the more remarkable. But when the travelers reach Hollin, a remnant of the Elvish atmosphere remains and they take some short-lived refuge in a hollow surrounded by holly bushes.

Holly was the token of the Elven-smiths, and in medieval herb lore it had magical protective powers against evil. It is seen in the fourteenth-century alliterative poem that Tolkien edited in Middle English and also translated, *Sir Gawain and the Green Knight,* which is written in the West Midlands dialect he loved. A fearsome Green Knight enters Arthur's hall during Christmas festivities with the intent of playing a beheading game to test the court. He appears bearing "a holyn bobbe þhat is grattest in grene when greuez ar bare" ("a holly-bundle that is greatest in greenery when groves are leafless"; 205)[10] as a sign of peace in one hand, and an enormous ax in the other. Although an olive branch was the traditional sign of peace, holly was (and is) associated with Christmas merriment and could signify wishes of joy and peace during the holiday, although it is in ironic juxtaposition to the knight's

HOLLY
Ilex aquifolium

weapon. The holly in Eregion is a vestige of happier days and although
the plants remain, Legolas tells his companions that the Elves, who left
for the Havens long ago, are forgotten by the grass and trees and are
lamented only by the stone that they mined.[11]

So far, we've seen several ways Tolkien used flora to create a sense of
verisimilitude in *The Lord of the Rings,* adding to the physical realism
and cultural depth. Up until Rivendell, the majority of the characters
and locales are within easy imagination; Elves are seen fleetingly and
introduced as majestic, wondrous beings, but not without human qualities. This portrayal is heightened at Rivendell but within a recognizable
setting, with halls, carved beams, and splendor reminiscent of a Keats
poem and medieval tapestries. But Lothlórien is different. The epitome
of beauty and enchantment, even in its loftiness it touches the heart.
Lothlórien is the thematic and emotional center of *The Lord of the*

Rings; it is there that pure joy and light are glimpsed, and the heartbreak of loss is comprehended. The sorrow that accompanies the coming of the Fourth Age and the passing of the Elves begins here, as does the understanding of the scope and urgency of the Quest.

Tolkien centered his vision of the ethereal home of High Elves on flora, but ordinary plant life obviously would not suffice; so he created flowers and trees of incomparable beauty reaching just beyond mortal vision. In Letter 312, he tries to liken *elanor* and *niphredil* to earthly plants—pimpernel for one, snowdrop for the other—but admits that they cannot be truly visualized.[12] Nor should we try to do so; it is better to feel their loveliness in the realm of longing and imagination, where they will never fade.

But the Lothlórien landscape contains sights familiar to medievals and moderns: grassy turf, flowery mead, enclosed garden and fountain. When the travelers' blindfolds are removed upon entering Cerin Amroth, they are dazzled by a carpet of green grass that covers a mound crowned by *mallorn* trees and then spreads to the hillsides, where it is sprinkled with flowers. Turves of fine grass have been prized for centuries before the modern mania for the perfect lawn, and hillocks that offer visual variety from flat expanses and provide seating and play areas are still popular. The vision of grass mixed with blooms starts in medieval gardens when pure turf is invaded by simple, tiny flowers like daisies, thyme, speedwell (veronica), and self-heal (prunella). In Lórien, the green of the grass is pure and fresh as if seen for the first time, and common blooms are replaced by *elanor* and *niphredil.* It is reminiscent of the flowery mead, in which many kinds of flowers join the turf to form a dense, colorful carpet and become the stylized *millefleurs* motif of medieval and Renaissance tapestries and art. The fountain that stands amid the lawn surrounding the home of Celeborn and Galadriel was an important feature of medieval pleasure and contemplative gardens, and the stream that issues forth from the fountain, leading to Galadriel's garden and mirror, conforms with traditional medieval design.

The term "enclosed garden" conjures many images and associations. The small pleasure garden, or herber, was recorded and detailed by Albertus Magnus in the late twelfth century; unlike the medicinal and kitchen garden, it was intended solely for enjoyment rather than utility. Filled with grass, fragrant herbs, and flowers and shaded by surrounding trees, it was a place for rest and aesthetic experience, and a fountain,

Flowers That Adorn

In *The Lord of the Rings,* as in all ages and cultures, flowers are found in many places other than gardens and woodlands, and they serve decorative and celebratory functions. Forget-me-nots grow not in the ground but on Goldberry's belt and in the blue of Tom's clothing. Arwen wears a silver girdle of leaves, and Lúthien's sleeves and mantle are sprinkled with golden blossoms. The Elven cloaks given to the members of the Company are fastened with brooches shaped like a green leaf veined with silver, and Galadriel's parting gifts to Merry and Pippin are belts with a clasp like a golden flower. Anduril's sheath is engraved with flowers and leaves in silver and gold, set with runes and gems. For her last meeting with the Fellowship, Galadriel wears a garland of blooms in her hair; such adornments were popular in medieval times not only for their fragrance and beauty but for symbolic and medicinal value. When Aragorn enters Minas Tirith as King Elessar, the folk have returned, filled their homes with flowers and music, and dressed in gay colors and floral garlands to greet him as he walks along the flower-lined streets. Life has returned to Gondor.

pool, or basin, was at its treeless center. A luxury, herbers were found at castles, manor houses, and monasteries. Reality merged with metaphor in the *hortus conclusus* image of art and literature, representing the eternal spring of the Garden of Eden and providing a site for courtly romance. In religious art, figures poised on a trellised herber seat, surrounded with appropriate symbolic flowers, like lilies and roses for Marian scenes. A great deal more could be said about the enclosed garden and *hortus conclusus,* but out of respect for Tolkien's detestation of allegory and his careful avoidance of theological implication, we will bypass the subject and look briefly at (not into) Galadriel's mirror.

The basin is fed by the fountain on the hill of Cerin Amroth and sits in a treeless green hollow that is enclosed by a hedge, much like an herber, though with a different function. Tolkien is cautious about the use of magic, and through Galadriel he places it apart from ordinary definition. For her, manipulation of forces and possession of sight into space beyond human reach are natural, but she doesn't understand mortals' perception of magic, especially since they apparently cannot discern between true and deceitful actions and visions.[13] While Tolkien sees magic as essentially neutral, he cites the former differentiation between *magia,* which was associated with "good," and *goeteia,* which bore connotations of "bad." Both Elves and the Enemy use both types, but with very different purpose and effect—artistry and beneficence by the former and destruction and deceit by the latter—which intersects with the larger theme of intent and motivation.[14] Frodo's and Sam's visions in the mirror may be oracular and their meanings clouded, but they reveal what is important to each. And for Sam, it is first his master and then home. Galadriel's "magic" parting gift to Sam enables him to restore the Shire to beauty and surpass his greatest gardening hope, by which Galadriel had tested him: a bit of garden of his own.

The grass of herber and mead becomes vast, rolling turf in Rohan. Fed by the Entwash, the fields and plains of Rohan are rimmed with pools, bogs, and sedge and fingered with rivulets filled with cresses and water plants. Imprints in the lush foliage of grass blades allow Strider, Gimli, and Legolas to pursue the Orc bands after the attack at the Falls of Rauros. The pungent, refreshing aroma of the grass gives new energy to their attempt to rescue Pippin and Merry, who escape into Fangorn Forest, which we will visit later.

When Aragorn, Gimli, and Legolas are redirected to Edoras by Gandalf, the companions cross fields of tall grasses, wet meads, and streams lined with willows, and as they approach the gates they pass the burial mounds of past rulers. The turf on the barrows is studded with white, starlike Evermind, which blooms on men's graves in all seasons. When Théoden joins his ancestors, his mound is planted with grass and Evermind. In the language of the Rohirrim, the flower is called *Simbelmynë,* which comes from Old English *simbel,* "continual, always," and *myne,* "remembrance, memorial." Human names in Rohan also have Old English derivation;

"ðēoden" is "prince, king," and "eoh" is "horse," so that names beginning with "eo" reflect the love of the animal.[15] (In *Beowulf*, Éomer translates to "help for horses."). As Legolas observes, the speech of Rohan is like its land: rich and rolling, yet hard and stern. As elsewhere, Tolkien created a language that describes its people and culture; a base of Old English evokes the world of *Beowulf*, a society based on *comitatus* values and valor, compared to the courtly world of Gondor. At the center of Rohan culture is Meduseld, King Théoden's splendid hall, with its mighty carved pillars and gold-thatched, lofty roof. It recalls Heorot, the "medo-ærn micel men gewyrcean," "heal-ærna mæst" ("gabled mead-hall fashioned by craftsmen," "greatest of hall buildings"; 69, 78) that is assailed by Grendel and defended by Beowulf. King Hrothgar's "heal-reced" ("royal building"; 68) "hlīfade," "hēah ond horn-gēap" ("towered high," "cliff-like, horn gabled"; 81–82).

The peoples of Middle-earth are culturally diverse, even within their own social and linguistic framework, including dialects. Differentiation in language causes separation and hampers cooperative relationships, and Tolkien solves the problem with Common Speech, although even Westron is marked with accents and chauvinistic variation. In "A Secret Vice," Tolkien expresses approval of the invented Esperanto, but as a means for distinguishing Europeans from non-Europeans, so that again there is a divisive element.[16] (He feels that Esperanto failed due to a lack of accompanying legends.[17]) There is a hierarchy of language in Middle-earth, with Elvish at the top, through the elevated speech of Gondor, to the rustic talk of Shire folk; in terms of aesthetics and context, Orcish is at the bottom, and the language of Mordor is virtually unspeakable to those outside that land. When Gandalf repeats the words inscribed on the One Ring at the Council of Elrond, he is upbraided by Elrond for daring to "utter words of that tongue" in Rivendell, where it had never before been spoken.[18]

Most people who use Common Speech in addition to their own language do so with fair fluency, even Orcs. There is one curious exception: the Woses, wild men of the Druadan Forest. Their headman, Ghân-buri-Ghân, speaks a broken Westron mixed with words from his own tongue. This qualifies as pidgin, in which the primary language frequently is that of the socially more powerful group; imperfect learning of the dominant language by the lesser group can lead to an image of cultural inferiority. Indeed, the Woses, who are depicted as crudely primitive, say they have been hunted like beasts, and their pulsating drums might evoke the disdain associated with the "uncivilized." Yet they are ancient and earth-wise; Théoden senses Ghân-buri-Ghân's shrewdness and awareness of events in his environment and accepts his offer to lead the Rohan host over forgotten paths to Minas Tirith.[19] The Woses prove trusty guides and guards, motivated by a hatred of Orcs and a desire to be allowed to live in the woods in peace. In reward, Aragorn gives the Forest of Druadan to them (something of an irony, since it has been their home for untold years), forbidden to Men. The Woses' imperfect Westron does not devalue or diminish their culture to those who look beyond speech to character. Regardless of status or placement in the language hierarchy of Middle-earth, everyone has potential for good or evil, wisdom or folly, and must face temptation and make choices. Even Saruman is given a chance to reform, which leads us to Isengard.

It would seem that there is little to study at Isengard on our botanical tour. But the absence of trees and plant life tells the tale of Saruman. The Wizard's Vale, which lies on the approach to Isengard, announces the despoliation of land and leaf under Saruman's rule. Once fertile and green, the valley is marred by charred stumps of felled trees and choked with weeds and brambles. As Gandalf, Théoden, and company ride through the once-pleasant place, they feel its sorrow and witness Saruman's malevolence through his cruelty to nature.

The orchards that once surrounded Isengard and Orthanc have been destroyed and replaced with stone and metal pillars by the corrupt wizard, and the plain has been tunneled to house and fuel the instruments of war. Isengard, once a stronghold of Gondor, is riddled with machines and fumes, imitating and foreshadowing Barad-dûr. Saruman's violation of nature is fittingly reversed by nature, as Treebeard and the Ents restore Isengard to a garden setting, and the path to Orthanc is bordered with living green and marked by sentinel trees. The Ents' toil and spirit bring a wholesomeness that attracts old and wild trees back to Isengard. When Aragorn has been crowned king, he grants the surrounding valley to the Ents for a new forest in reparation for the trees lost at the hands of "Tree-killer" Saruman and his servants.

It is March when Saruman is defeated and the Company departs. Tolkien's careful attention to time, weather, and season contributes greatly to creating realism in Middle-earth; consistent chronology is an important unifying element in the multistranded narrative of *The*

HAWTHORN

Lord of the Rings, and Tolkien kept complex maps and calendars as he wrote to track events and the movements of the characters. Plant life, of course, is tied to climate and seasonal cycles and serves as an indicator of the time of year as well as the essence of a place. When Legolas, Gimli, and Aragorn enter Rohan, they are invigorated by the soft, warm air and scent of spring, winter seemingly left behind. Rivendell has the feel of summer in autumn, and the beauty of Lórien in winter fills the heart so that there is no longing for spring or summer.

The Company's first stop after Isengard is a dale nestled against the foot of Dol Baran. Among last year's dried bracken leaves that they gather for fire fuel, new fronds bring the sight and smell of spring. The hawthorn under which they find shelter is one of spring's earliest har-bingers, and the old treelike shrubs and bushes under which they camp are welcoming the new season with bright green leaf buds. Hawthorn, or quickthorn, is well suited for the scene; it grows in dense, windproof thorny thickets and is used as a hedge in the country to protect and

BRACKEN
Pteridium aquilinum

contain livestock. The blossoms are considered unlucky even today and have been associated with the smell of death: not fancifully, since they contain a substance that is also produced in decaying human tissue. But the hawthorn has also had medicinal and culinary uses, as well as powers protective against evil. So it would provide a perfect natural haven for the travelers.

Frodo and Sam are far less fortunate in finding shelter after leaving the Falls of Rauros and heading for Mordor. The rocky cliffs and crevices of the Emyn Muil, with their sparse vegetation of stunted and dead trees that barely hint at once having been healthy, offer no cover. The hobbits sleep on cold stone for two nights before finally escaping the inhospitable clefts that bar their progress. Gollum has little difficulty negotiating the sheer walls but still is snared by Sam and becomes an unwilling (and wily) guide. They fare little better under his direction as he leads them to the Dead Marshes, the eerie atmosphere of which is announced by hissing dry reeds that rattle although the air is still. They thread their way around disgusting bogs and pools and crouch for rest in grasses and reeds that, like the faces in the slimy marsh, are dead and rotting.

But the stench and decay of the Dead Marshes do not prepare Frodo and Sam for their first shocking view of the country that leads to Mordor. The hobbits face a grey, barren, and polluted wasteland, and they are stricken with the horror of Sauron's devastation that is manifested in the complete absence—or hope—of any plant life. The land is a hideous perversion of Lothlórien: it will never see spring or summer again. Of all the signs of the Enemy's evil, the destruction of flora is the most dramatic and damning.

Nevertheless, they continue their journey to the Gates of Moria, through Cirith Gorgor, the Haunted Pass. Like other previous sites of the Free Peoples' strength and glory, the towers guarding the entrance to Mordor have been overtaken by Sauron, and the dignity and honor they once represented have been replaced with malice. But his destructive reach is limited, and when the hobbits are blocked at the Black Gates and detoured by Gollum toward Cirith Ungol and Shelob's Lair, they first pass through Ithilien, the Garden of Gondor. Although its vigor waned with that of Gondor, Ithilien still possesses powers of protection and healing that emanate from its trees, herbs, and blooms. It is so rich in flora that it deserves a separate chapter, which follows in the next chapter.

Before reaching the stairs of Cirith Ungol, the hobbits pass over a stream whose banks are carpeted with luminous white flowers. But unlike the meads in Lothlórien, the loveliness of the blooms is corrupted, and they are repugnant to sight and smell. Before Frodo and Sam disappear into the darkness of Shelob's Lair, they have a few moments that dispel hopelessness, however briefly. On the border of Ithilien, Sam comes across the site of a recent fire, strewn with bones and skulls. Although he is repulsed by the horrific scene, we see that it is being reclaimed by wild briar, clematis, and eglantine as nature survives and even surmounts the carnage. Later, at the Cross Roads where they turn toward Cirith Ungol, the stone head that has fallen from the defiled statue of an ancient king is encircled with blossoming vines. The natural crown gives Frodo a fleeting sign that good cannot be permanently overcome, and the yellow stonecrop that forms living hair beneath the flowering garland has found its favorite habitat of old stone and turns a symbol of desecration into one of hope. When Aragorn and his host pass the Cross Roads on the way to Mordor and battle, the Orc head that had been set on the statue is broken and replaced with the ancient king's, still crowned with plant wreaths, a sign of the restoration to come. *The Lord of the Rings* is far too complex to be reduced to a simple tale of good versus evil, but one of the questions that must be asked is whether it is ultimately optimistic or pessimistic. Tolkien explores the issue in many places, not least in his botany, where he directs our gaze toward the ephemeral beauty of a single bloom and the enduring strength of nature.

CHAPTER 3

ITHILIEN

The Garden of Gondor

ENGLISH BLUEBELL
Hyacinthoides non-scripta

hroughout their adventures, the fellow travelers move from danger to haven, although the safe places encompass more potential hazard as the journey progresses, and Ithilien might have been the most dangerous of all. Unlike other significant havens such as the house of Tom Bombadil, Rivendell, and Lothlórien, Ithilien has no supernatural magic. Rather, its power to revive and heal comes from remnants of grace left from its past greatness, and its own earthly magic that comes from its flora.

Turning aside from the ghastly sight of Mordor, Frodo, Sam, and Gollum enter the borders of the fair country of Ithilien. The wholesome air and sweet scent immediately refresh Sam and remind him of the Shire, while Gollum nearly chokes. During their brief stay in Ithilien, the weight of the Ring becomes lighter and Frodo is able to have peaceful sleep. Their time there is short, but eventful.

The initial refreshment Frodo and Sam feel is enhanced by the comfort and nourishment of the rabbit stew Sam prepares; as in happier days, he's a campfire cook, using his utensils and hobbit culinary skills. The smoke from the fire attracts Faramir and his company, who guard Ithilien and Gondor from threatening forces. The hobbits' apparent danger worsens dramatically when Sam slips and tells his captors about the Ring. Faramir has just been introduced, but his personality is rapidly developed, and we meet the only character in *The Lord of the Rings* besides Bombadil who is not tempted by the Ring.

The site of impending peril becomes a testing ground for trust; Faramir and Frodo must rely on each other's honor in order to maintain their safety and commitments. The tactic Frodo uses to save Gollum appears to be a betrayal to Sméagol and fuels the dark side of his (unevenly) divided nature, on which Frodo and Sam must once again depend. The rituals that accompany Faramir's judiciary pronouncements and the rendering of Gollum into Frodo's care recall medieval cultural custom and values, particularly *trouthe,* a concept of utmost importance reflected in the literature Tolkien studied. More than just truth, among its many facets were trust, fidelity in love and friendship, honor and integrity, and devotion and loyalty, and it underlies the basis of Frodo and Faramir's relationship. Oath-keeping was an essential element of *trouthe,* which is shown in Frodo's refusal to break faith after he has given Gollum his word, despite the possible consequences and Faramir's warnings, and in the extraction of an oath from Gollum not to reveal the location or existence of the Forbidden Pool.[1] The Dead who follow Aragorn into battle do so to fulfill a broken oath and thus find peace, and old oaths and friendship bind Rohan to Gondor when called upon as the siege of Minas Tirith looms. Even Sméagol/Gollum feels bound to keep the oath he had sworn on the Ring to aid and obey Frodo, articulated in his debate over the sleeping hobbit whether to remain faithful to his promise and master, or to take his Precious and become Gollum the Great.[2]

Ithilien is not forgotten when the hobbits leave it behind, continue their journey, and ultimately fulfill their Quest. When Sam awakes after being rescued from Mt. Doom by Gwaihir and taken to Ithilien, he recognizes the aroma of the place and momentarily thinks himself still cooking coneys. Aragorn's powers heal Sam and Frodo and bring them back from darkness, and Ithilien provides an atmosphere in which all can rest and feel joy after their long toils and trials. The victory over Sauron is celebrated on the Field of Cormallen, where Frodo and Sam are honored and Sam's wish for the singing of a lay that tells of their adventures comes true. The members of the Fellowship are reunited, and their labors come to fruition: Aragorn's kingship and the beginning of the Fourth Age.

In establishing his reign Aragorn continues the Stewardship of Gondor, and Faramir is given Ithilien as a princedom, where he and Éowyn will live. The ancient land, located between Mordor and Gondor, was beleaguered as Sauron regained power. Abandoned by its original inhabitants, it remains desolate yet lovely until Sauron is overthrown. Although under Sauron's dominion for only a short time and never completely contaminated by him, Ithilien is still haunted by the Enemy's malice, but the forest becomes a home for Legolas and Silvan Elves and is once again the Garden of Gondor. But we are reminded that these Elves, like the others, eventually will yield to the call of the sea and depart, and the Age of Man is tinged with the sorrow of loss.

Ithilien gives us a glance at Tolkien's perception of himself as subcreator of Middle-earth. In his letters, he repeatedly describes characters and events as having a separate life, which is revealed to and through him as a reporter rather than inventor. For example, in Letter 66 he says that Faramir appeared unbidden and unwanted, although liked; he simply came walking into Ithilien.[3] The country seems to have unfolded itself and become a lovely place as Tolkien worked, as though without conscious design. However, the plant life demonstrates a very clear vision; whether Tolkien made deliberate choices or drew on instinct and inspiration, the result is a landscape filled with the perfect flora to enliven that vision. Less lofty or awesome than Lórien, Ithilien is more immediately and easily visualized and sensed through the sight and scent of familiar plants and the pleasure of their heartening effects.

On the borders and in the vale where the travelers spend time, there are over thirty trees, shrubs, flowers, and other plants; many are recognizable, but there are some that Sam the gardener cannot identify, expanding the floral world beyond known bounds for a sense of depth beneath surface narrative. The beauty of spring in the woods of Ithilien is depicted in a dense, brief space in the style of a medieval or epic catalog, overwhelming the reader and hobbits with a panoply of texture, color, and fragrance, which we will try to evoke here. Once again, Tolkien shares a philosophical attitude with William Morris and his followers in a love of natural settings. Gertrude Jekyll, one of Morris's chief continuators, observed the wild beauty of a moorland that she felt would be spoiled by the addition of common nursery plants as proposed.[4] She believed in respecting individual localities and flora, and if one wished to enhance existing natural gardens, she recommended broom, rosemary, lavender, and other indigenous plants that would resonate with Tolkien's imaginary landscape.

A love of woodland appears early in Tolkien's art career, which he began by sketching and drawing under his mother's tutelage at Sarehole, where they lived for four years, from 1896 to 1900; he cherished the memory of the village and mill, which is recalled in Hobbiton. Over the years, in works like *Foxglove Year* and *The Cottage* (1913) and *Spring* (1940), Tolkien recorded his enjoyment of the seasons, gardens, and trees in his art. When he illustrated *The Hobbit* and *The Lord of the Rings,* he filled Middle-earth with wooded landscapes in places like Rivendell, Mirkwood, Lothlórien, and the hall of the King of the Wood Elves.

Ithilien is Tolkien's master achievement of woodland creation. Spring is a traditionally welcome time, dispelling the cold darkness of winter:

The rose raileth hire rode,
The leves on the lighte wode
    Waxen al with wille.

The moone mandeth hire blee,
The lilie is lofsom to see,
    The fenil and the fille.
                "Spring," c. 1330
The rose reveals her redness,
The leaves on bright wood
    Grow with joy.
The moon casts her light,
The lily is lovely to see,
    The fennel and the thyme.

Tolkien tells of an April morning at home on Northmoor Road when the mist lifts and reveals the "silver light of spring" that shone on newly leafing quince, apple, and hawthorn, accompanied by a "marvelous show" of narcissus.[5]

The season is bursting forth in Ithilien when Frodo and Sam arrive in March, and it is doubly comforting after the lifelessness of Mordor. Virtually all the plants they see are prized as early heralds of the season and for their aroma. Many are native to Britain, and most nonnatives had been introduced so long ago that they were common in medieval times. Few lacked medicinal or culinary uses, and many found their way into homes as decoration and to bring in the sweet smell of springtime. And for Sam and Frodo, they bring the last bit of respite until they fulfill their Quest and return to Ithilien.

Rather than taking a panoramic view, the best way to experience Ithilien is to accompany the hobbits during their visit. As soon as they approach Ithilien, they find the land improved and are greeted with the fragrance of pine and the hues of heather, broom, and cornel that sweep the heathland. Heather, of course, is native to that terrain, and Tolkien denotes the plant's ancient history by calling it ling, the name derived from an Old English word for fire and given to the plant in Anglo-Saxon times, when it was used for fuel. Aromatic mattresses were made from ling, so it's not surprising that Frodo sleeps peacefully in the heather where the hobbits take shelter. While heather blooms are occasionally white, which are considered lucky, they are usually purple, a lively contrast to the yellow flowers of broom.

Broom also has a long pedigree. Known as *Planta genista,* it is said to have given the Plantaganets their name from the sprig of broom that Geoffrey, Count of Anjou, wore in his hat. Broom had magical properties, used both by and against witches, particularly in matters of love. In a thirteenth-century poem, a wife seeks advice from a spirit in a broom bush:

Tell me, being in the broom,
Teach me what to do
That my husband
Love me true.

She is told,

When your tongue is still,
You'll have your will.[6]

Common broom is still seen today, although it's thought to be unlucky in the house, and grows in beautiful masses of bright blooms and vivid green foliage in springtime. Like many shrubs, it provides food for insects like bees and caterpillars and shelter for small mammals and birds, reminding us that plants are part of the vast ecological system. Both broom and heather served many functions in the medieval household, including use as brooms, in leather tanning, and in clothing dyes; paper was made from broom bark, and ale was flavored with heather.

Wild heather and broom are easily identified and envisioned, while their companion, cornel, is somewhat trickier. The *Cornus*, or dogwood, can be a shrub or a small tree, and many varieties bloom in spring. Morris admired the pretty white flowers on a tree that bloomed along with hawthorn at the site of his workshop at Merton Abbey, where he treasured the natural settings of meadows, river banks, and carpets of violets and primroses in spring. He was unfamiliar with the tree, and when told it was a dogwood, he was unable to find it in the seminal botanist's handbook, Gerard's late sixteenth-century *Herball*,[7] probably because dogwoods were introduced to Britain from other countries. However, Culpeper lists the yellow-blossomed cornel (dogberry) tree in his *Complete Herbal*, and he recommends a syrup of the berries for stomach ailments and hysterical fits.[8] Legend tells that the berries that Circe fed to Odysseus's men to turn them into pigs were from the dogwood. Like many plants brought into Britain, the cornel has become absorbed into the landscape, but there is a native dogwood, the *Cornus sanguinea,* which is still grown today as a hedgerow shrub. It is less spectacular than some imported varieties but has a lush red coloring to its stems, especially in winter, and creamy white flowers in late spring and summer. So, depending on which cornel Tolkien had in mind, we have a choice of white or yellow blooms to complete the picture of the heathland that leads to Ithilien.

After resting in the heather, the hobbits strike an ancient road that heads south and that is flanked by weeds, moss, trees, bracken, and more ling. As they come closer to Ithilien, the air becomes sweeter, and at the end of the road they have a vista of the Garden of Gondor: slopes and vales covered with trees, shrubs, flowers, and other plants. Sheltered from the chill of north and east, the flora thrives in the warmth from the south and west, and birdsong greets the season. There is a profusion of greens; the bright new foliage of awakening deciduous trees and ferns mingles with deep shades of evergreen trees like the fir and cypress, and the silvery tones of the olive. Feathery, leathery, flat, and bushy shapes and textures blend and hover above a carpet of moss, mold, and turf.

An abundance of herbs adds to the color palette and gives pungency to the fragrance of the resinous trees. Even Sam cannot identify all the herbs that crowd the ground and steal along crevices, but several are known to most readers, though perhaps not in their natural state. Thyme, marjoram, and sage were used for centuries as medicinal cure-alls and culinary flavorings, and in cosmetics, potpourris, and perfumes, and each had special properties. In Greek, *thymus* meant both "courage" and "fumigate"; medieval ladies embroidered thyme on the favors they gave to knights for bravery, and common thyme (*Thymus vulgaris*) was used to rid houses of pests. Because fairies favored its flower, thyme was reputed to have the power to make them visible to humans. The marjoram growing in Ithilien could be the *Origanum vulgare* (wild marjoram or Greek oregano) which, like sage and thyme, was introduced into England by the Romans. An ancient sign of peace, it was worn by bride and groom and planted on graves to bring rest to the dead. It might also be the sweet marjoram (*Origanum majorana*) brought to Britain during the Middle Ages, which served as a preservative, disinfectant, and furniture polish in addition to more fragrant uses. *Salvia* (for which Salvia Bolger was named) derives from *salvare,* to heal or save, and *salvus,* in recognition of its medicinal properties. Sage (*Salvia officinalis*) was believed to possess the power of longevity; depending on its vigor in the garden, sage could predict the success or failure of a business, and in modern times its

$\mathcal{S}$ALVIA
$\mathcal{S}$alvia coccinea

growth is still thought to be an indicator of the dominant partner in a marriage.[9]

While March might be too early for thyme or marjoram to yield the pink, purple, red, white, and other colored blossoms loved by bees and butterflies, their foliage, often prized for its own sake, would add dimension to the scene. Both plants come in many varieties, mounding to spreading, with leaves ranging from green to silver to gold, solid to variegated, smooth to woolly. There are hundreds of varieties of salvia, native to many lands, some of which bloom in spring (each season has varieties in blossom), and those seen by Sam and Frodo are already showing blue, red, and pale green flowers.[10]

Parsley grows along with the other herbs, and it may be the *Petroselinum crispum* that, like the others, was a staple in medieval herb and medicinal gardens. Its curly leaves and bright green color would be a good partner for the thyme, marjoram, and sage. There is another "parsley" that would be equally at home in Ithilien: the *Anthriscus sylvestris,* cow parsley, or Queen Anne's lace. It's a common weed that thrives in hedgerows, roadsides, and woodlands, and its lacey white blooms float atop long, slender stems and fernlike leaves in spring. It also brings to mind the imagery of the Lúthien lay:

The leaves were long, the grass was green,
    The hemlock-umbrels tall and fair,
And in the glade a light was seen
    Of stars in shadow shimmering.[11]

Tolkien depicts the scene of his visits with Edith in the woodland glade that inspired the myth as filled with "hemlock" or a similar plant with white umbelliferous blooms[12] (clearly not the hemlock tree); this is a perfect description of cow parsley, which is related to the poisonous hemlock and cowbane family and very similar in appearance, but nontoxic. The clouds of delicate blooms and foliage would cast an ethereal air on both Yorkshire and Ithilien glades.

The stony walls of Ithilien contrast with the lushness of the herbal bouquet, but they, too, are showing signs of spring. It's always amazing to see plants clinging to life on rocks, a seemingly inhospitable environment for flora. Yet plants like stonecrop, which help reanimate the fallen king's head at the Cross Roads, and saxifrage flourish in such places. The genus *saxifraga* is enormous and includes alpine plants, which thrive in rocky spots. Generally low growers, they form dense mats, and some offer bright blooms in spring. But even without blossoms, the green or silver foliage joins with the yellow stonecrop to add to the spring tapestry of Ithilien.

Cow Parsley
Anthriscus sylvestris

That medley of color becomes glorious where budding primeroles and anemones emerge between the filberts, and asphodel and lilies sprinkle the grass. The primerole is a rather mysterious flower; it is usually assumed to be a primrose, but early literary references are unclear and the name may have referred to cowslip (perhaps including the primula) or the field daisy. We will assume that it is the primrose here, and as we

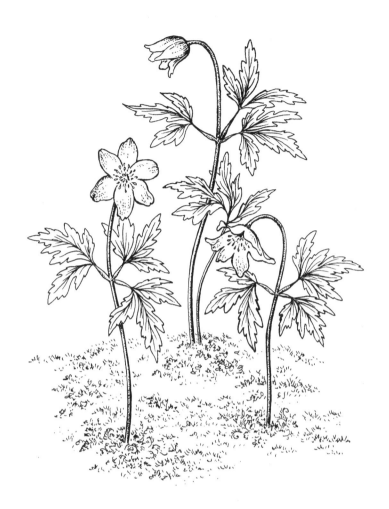

Wood ~ Anemone
Anemone nemorosa

saw with Primula Baggins, its yellow blooms are among spring's earliest. The anemone also poses a slight identification problem; most were introduced to Europe from Asia in the sixteenth century and were widely cultivated, but they don't quite fit the Ithilien spirit despite their early spring blossoming and tendency to naturalize, even where unwanted in gardens. Rather, we may envision the native wood anemone, the signifier of ancient woodlands, with its white, yellow, purple, blue, or scarlet

A S P H O D E L

blossoms spreading through the turf. Combined with the yellow primroses, the setting recalls one enjoyed by Tolkien in March at the Fellows'
Garden of Merton College; he likened the scene with its blue anemones,
butterflies above bright green grass, and purple, white, and yellow cro-
cuses to a Pre-Raphaelite picture.[13]

Asphodel may be Tolkien's most curious plant selection, since it is not
native to Britain or woodland, although it appears in old border gardens.
The choice may have been based on the mythic lore surrounding the
plant. Also known as King's Spear, the name comes from a Greek word

meaning scepter, but moreover the plant was associated by the ancients with death and renewed life and was planted near tombs and graves; a favorite food of the dead, it was said to fill Hades and the Elysian Fields. This symbolism appears in poetry from Homer to William Carlos Williams, and if we stretch the image of death and rebirth, it might reach far enough to encompass the spring cycle. Or, perhaps Tolkien simply liked the name and/or flower; he did give it to Asphodel Burrows, Frodo's aunt. It is a lilaceous plant, with white and yellow blooming varieties, either of which would be good company for the lilies and other flowers of the Ithilien floral fabric.

The hobbits follow a stream and come to a lake formed in an ancient stone basin, now covered with moss and wild roses, and the refreshing pond is punctuated by iris and water lilies. Here we are reminded of Goldberry, who sits amid bowls of floating blossoms from the river and wears a gold belt shaped of flag lilies. The iris in Ithilien are undoubtedly the common yellow flag, *Iris pseudacorus;*[14] also known as Flower-de-luce, it was adopted by Louis VII as the "fleur de Louis" during the second crusade and is the source of the French fleur-de-lys. The water-loving plant has a bright bloom in spring, and the freshness of the maiden in *Pearl* is compared to the "flor-de-lys" (IV:195). A common plant for medievals, it yielded yellow dye and ink, and iris generally were believed to ward off evil spirits. Culpeper found the scent unpleasant when green but improved with drying, and he reports its use in sweet-bags and perfumes in addition to medicinal effects against pestilential contagion and noxious air.[15] In the twentieth century, biting the plant was believed to cause speech impediments, and the long, spiked leaves are still made into boats by children.[16]

The spot where the hobbits settle for rest provides Sam with the chance to tend to the hunger for homely food he felt since entering the woods. Once Gollum supplies the rabbits, Sam uses dried bracken for fuel as did medievals, who also used the ashes of the burnt fronds in glassmaking and as soap and fertilizer. The cedar branches from the surrounding trees that Sam adds to the fire gives it a sweet aroma, and there are plentiful herbs for flavoring the stew: thyme, marjoram, bay, and sage. Although missing the vegetables that would grow later in the year, like turnips, potatoes, and wild carrot (that still grows in hedgerows), the stew and its broth satisfy the need for both food and comfort. Rosemary, symbol of remembrance and friendship, is not listed in the

YELLOW IRIS
Iris pseudacorus

Ithilien inventory, although it can easily be imagined among the tangle
of herbs and in the stew pot. There are a few common plants, including
herbs and flowers, that are not included in Tolkien's botanical choices

throughout *The Lord of the Rings* that might be expected, such as the fragrant, useful sweet violet; lavender, ubiquitous in medieval and modern gardens; foxgloves, which he illustrated and investigated the Anglo-Saxon etymology of the name, citing the old herbals;[17] and the deep blue cornflower, which forms the design of the heraldic device for Idril, Eärendil's mother.[18]

After meeting with Faramir and passing through the woods, the hobbits see a final sweep of beauty in expanses of turf mixed with white and blue anemones, blue and purple woodland hyacinth, and yellow celandine. The woodland hyacinth, *Hyacinthoides non-scripta*, is not the stocky, often overwhelmingly aromatic flower we see today that was originally imported from the Turkish Empire and developed into cultivars, but the British native bluebell. Its slender stalks are covered with small bell-shaped blooms that are spectacular in dense, seemingly endless carpets. Nestled at their base is the lesser celandine (*Ranunculus ficaria*), in a mat of bright blooms that display its membership in the buttercup family. As they move out of the Ithilien woodlands, the flora becomes more sparse and less welcoming, although the yellow, faintly scented gorse (also known as furze and whin) still greets spring, and the blackberry bramble that lines the thorn bushes in which they take shelter is also awakening. Finally, they must leave the havenlike atmosphere and loveliness of Ithilien and proceed to the Cross Roads, the darkness and terror of Cirith Ungol and Mt. Doom looming ahead.

The Cross Roads is circled with trees that Tolkien does not identify, unlike his catalog of trees in Ithilien: fir, cedar, cypress, terebinth, olive, bay, juniper, myrtle, filbert, oak, ash, and others known and unknown to the travelers. For the most part, description and discussion of these trees have been skirted in our view of Ithilien in order to focus on the plants closer at hand while walking through the woods. And many trees are familiar to the reader and need less attention than the flora that may be new to someone unfamiliar with medieval plants, cottage gardens, or woodlands. But Tolkien loved trees and felt a strong connection to them; at age seventy-one, he likened his feelings to "an old tree that is losing all its leaves one by one."[19] Trees have a central place in his creative imagination as well as in the plot, narrative technique, imagery, and mythology of *The Lord of the Rings,* which he called his "own internal Tree."[20] They are honored as the home of Elves, the source of the Silmarils' light, and the White Tree of Gondor, memorial of the Eldar, and they provide shelter and support, pose danger, and represent hope. From the malevolent Old Man Willow to the magnificent *mallorn,* individually and in forests, trees are essential to the atmosphere and action and guide us on the next stage of our travels through Middle-earth.

CHAPTER 4

FORESTS AND TREES

CRACK WILLOW ~ *Salix fragilis*

any of Tolkien's early watercolors and sketches, taken from natural settings, feature trees; they dominate or dot landscapes, nestle against buildings, and even foreground cityscapes. Later, his awareness of contemporary art included fairy tale and children's books illustrators, and Arthur Rackham's trees seem to have had some influence, including on Old Man Willow.[1] In his illustrations for *The Hobbit* and *The Lord of the Rings,* Tolkien's renderings of forests and trees become more stylized than naturalistic and still frequently dominate the composition. Tree becomes pure design in *The Tree of Amalion,* which he drew often when he felt "driven to pattern-designing."[2] Its graceful, arching branches bear many different flowers, and while it may recall "sinuous Art nouveau-inspired flora,"[3] it is also strongly related to medieval manuscript illumination, where the same shapes and delicate blooms are a frequent element of border design.

Tree imagery is a repeated motif in Tolkien's clarification of literary creation. In "On Fairy-stories," a lecture later expanded into an essay, he encourages students to add their own leaves to the Tree of Tales, for no matter how dense the foliage from previous stories, there is newness and uniqueness in every leaf and each spring;[4] as in Bilbo's song, "in every wood in every spring, there is a different green."[5] It has often been remarked that "Leaf by Niggle," written at the same time as "On Fairy-stories" and while *The Lord of the Rings* was forming, is a reflection of Tolkien's creative process and his struggle to balance the exploration and expression of his imaginative life with his scholarly and societal commitments. His letters, themselves an enormous consumer of time and energy, are full of references to difficulty preparing and completing translations, editions, and other publishing projects in addition to his teaching and domestic duties, while wrestling with the call of Middle-earth. Though well meaning, Niggle begrudgingly attempted to meet his obligations but was only partially successful and resented the interruptions that took him away from his painting. It is easy to see a bit of Niggle in Tolkien, who was always overextended and behind schedule, and the success of *The Hobbit* and *The Lord of the Rings* added to the burden.

Niggle and Tolkien certainly shared similarities in their artistic work; Niggle toiled over every leaf and was never satisfied, as Tolkien labored over every detail, constantly revising and reworking. ("Leaf by Niggle" was an exception, which appeared to him completely composed upon awakening one morning, with no need for conscious effort or rewriting. The story was partly motivated by the sight of a great poplar tree that he could see from his bed, which was suddenly "lopped and dismembered" by its owner and eventually cut down, mourned only by Tolkien and two owls.[6]) There was always another "leaf" to Tolkien's literary tree, another "untold story" that took on a life of its own, just as birds appeared in Niggle's tree and a landscape surrounded it. Soon both men's creations grew beyond scope and manageability but became ever more intriguing and demanding, which placed greater strain on other responsibilities and challenged the place of art in the pragmatic world.

In "Leaf by Niggle," Tolkien examines the value of artistic work in utilitarian and aesthetic terms; ironically, his professional career depended on his relationship to, and utilization of, the imaginative product of poets. The debate over utilitarianism versus the imagination that accompanied the Industrial Revolution is reminiscent of Dickens's *Hard Times,* and Tolkien attempts a synthesis. While art can serve a useful purpose (other than patching a leaking roof with a painting as Niggle should have done to help his neighbor, Parish, during the storm and flood[7]) such as posters, it can also be appreciated for its own sake, the benefits of which are realized in the healing nature of Niggle's country and Parish's garden, the lovely manifestation of Niggle's imagined tree and landscape. Synthesis is also seen in the combination of creative activity and life management Niggle achieves, and symbiosis draws him and Parish together as one man imagines and the other implements. In the end, each realizes he had failed to recognize or appreciate the other's attributes, mostly out of self-absorption in life's exigencies.

There are many deep implications in "Leaf by Niggle," which is perhaps more demonstrative of Tolkien's philosophy of the fairy tale than his essay "On Fairy-stories," but most instructive here is the imagery of perpetually unfolding space and the independent, seemingly autonomous life of the creative process, symbolized by the Great Tree. Even after it is finished and Niggle's visions have become incarnate, there is still work to be done on the constantly materializing forest, lakes, gardens and, eventually for Niggle, the far-off mountains. His and Tolkien's curiosity and creative impetus are never-ending.

LOMBARDY POPLAR

Populus nigra betulifolia

Tolkien's love of trees began in his youth, at least as early as Sarehole. Carpenter recounts Tolkien's story of the senseless felling of a willow tree that he had loved to climb, an experience never forgotten.[8] "Leaf by Niggle" appeared in 1945, but trees had been at the center of his imagination much longer. For example, the poem "From the many-willow'd margin of the immemorial Thames" appeared in 1913, and "Light as Leaf on Linden-tree," the precursor of the tale of Tinúviel told by Strider at Weathertop, was published in 1925. In *The Lord of the Rings,* as with the other flora of Middle-earth, many trees are familiar, bringing connotations of special properties and lore to the literary landscape and stirring cultural memory. So do Tolkien's created trees, through their invented history and symbolism. For him, forests have their own nature, both formed by and reacting to events and influences. In Letter 339 he attributes the beauty of Lothlórien to the love felt for its trees, and the hostility of the Old Forest to injuries it has sustained. Likewise, Fangorn responds to the threat of destruction, and Mirkwood's spirit is infiltrated by evil.[9] These depictions attribute an innate personality to forests and individual trees, some of which are helpless to combat adverse forces, while others fight back. Not all trees in Middle-earth are animated. Frequently they are unidentified and form part of the landscape and occasionally serve functional purposes as landmarks, vantage points, protection from weather and visibility, sleeping quarters, safety from attack, and even battering rams as used by the Orcs at Helm's Deep. But many have independent life, and all deserve respect. Tolkien was horrified by the modern "torture and murder" of trees,[10] and in his literature he empowers them with great potential for action, good and bad.

Mirkwood

Mirkwood, which appears in *The Hobbit,* is the forerunner of the great forests in *The Lord of the Rings* and is one of the many cultural inheritances bequeathed to us through Tolkien. Most readers are not familiar with the forest's origin, but its spirit lives in Middle-earth. In the *Elder Edda,* Mirkwood is the mysterious area that lies between the lands of the warring Huns and Gjukings (Niflungs) through which warriors pass into enemy territory. The sound of "hooves of high-spirited horses / hammered the heath of Mirkwood the Unknown" (*The Lay of Atli,* stanza 13),[11] and the magic and danger of the valkyries, "maidens [who] flew from the south through Mirkwood, / young and wise, on their way to wars" (*The Lay of Volund*, stanza 1)[12] reverberate in the atmosphere of Tolkien's Mirkwood.

It may be disappointing to some that not all of Tolkien's creation is "original," but it must be remembered that the insistence on originality and the fear of plagiarism is quite modern. Medieval literature depended upon the recasting of existing works to suit the redactor's purpose and taste. Tolkien's use of sources like the Eddas and *Beowulf* is within that tradition, and it proves the importance of appropriation as a cultural continuum that preserves and transmits the beauty, values, and ideas of our predecessors. And, of course, Tolkien blends those elements with his own into a work of unique genius.

Tolkien's Mirkwood is perhaps even more fearsome than the Eddic, for it is the site of the renewal of the Enemy's power. According to the *Silmarillion*, the forest was once Greenwood the Great, the realm of Legolas's father, Thranduil, king of the Silvan Elves, and home to many beasts and birds. But upon returning to Middle-earth, Sauron moved into the south of the forest to regain his strength. Darkness and evil creatures came with him, and fear permeated the woods; only the north, under King Thranduil, resisted. It was the Shadow of Sauron, the sign of his return, but at first the change in Greenwood the Great was only observed and not identified, and the forest became known as Mirkwood.

At this time, the wizards arrived in Middle-earth: Saruman, Gandalf, and Radagast. Only Gandalf was vigilant enough to suspect the source of the Shadow and chased Sauron from Dol Guldur, the dark hill where the Enemy practiced his sorcery. But the peace was short-lived and Sauron returned to Mirkwood, increasing his power. Again, Gandalf discovered the Enemy's presence and strength, and the White Council attacked Dol Guldur; although Sauron was driven out, he had gathered great forces and, united against the Elves and the surviving Númenóreans, moved to Mordor and rebuilt Barad-Dûr. After Sauron's defeat in the War of the Rings, Thranduil reestablished his northern realm, and Mirkwood, renamed Eryn Lasgalen (Wood of Greenleaves), flourished. The Beornings and Woodmen were given the forest between the north and south territories, and for a time Celeborn took the southern part of the forest, renamed East Lórien, but he departed and few of his folk or their happiness remained behind.

The *Silmarillion* is often read (if at all) after *The Hobbit* and *The Lord of the Rings*, in which the *Silmarillion* myths are manifested. Although

Christopher Tolkien compiled and edited it, Tolkien never completed his "myth for England" that drove the creation of his literary works. Like Niggle's tree, the *Silmarillion* was constantly expanding and revealing new horizons, and one wonders whether it ever could have been finished. As published, it is a rather hefty tome filled with the legends of Middle-earth and beyond, which either never appear elsewhere save occasional enigmatic references, and/or are not always consistent with versions that do appear, and its recitals in Tolkien's letters are often more murky than illuminating.

While the history of characters like Gandalf and Galadriel, places like Mirkwood, and events before the Third Age supplies fascinating enhancement, it is not essential for an understanding or appreciation of the published literature, which Tolkien crafted so fully and carefully that it stands alone without the need for apocryphal material. Tolkien, of course, would see the situation reversed, since the *Silmarillion* was his main passion and all else secondary, but ironically it is in *The Hobbit* and *The Lord of the Rings* that the mythology is most accessible and enjoyable for many.

Even without knowing the background of Mirkwood from the *Silmarillion,* it is still a very frightening place. *The Hobbit,* a fairy tale written for children, is quite different from *The Lord of the Rings,* which Tolkien realized early was not for children as he saw it grow in artistic and philosophical complexity. But despite the light-hearted narrative of *The Hobbit,* the dark peril of Mirkwood threatens. Events in the forest touch upon characters and elements developed more fully in *The Lord of the Rings,* such as the revelation, both to the self and others, of one's hidden attributes, the possibility of little folk doing great deeds, and the dynamics of comradeship as the Company must cooperate to survive.

The trees of Mirkwood, mainly the beech and oak favored by the Wood-elves, are benign, but Beorn, who lives at the edge of the forest, warns of other dangers, all of which come true: lack of food and water, the black stream that brings sleep and forgetfulness, the dark shadows that lead to disorientation, and wild creatures. The spiders that nearly feast on Thorin and company foreshadow Shelob, although Tolkien's choice of spiders seems to be based on the universal fear of the creatures rather than personal dislike, since he mentions rescuing them from his bathtub.[13] Danger of another sort appears with the Wood-elves that divert and eventually capture the adventurers, though they also rescue

Tolkien's majestic Elves may be his most glorious creation and are, of course, quite different from traditional depictions, particularly in the late nineteenth century when elves and fairies were pictured on buttercup petals, and he regretted using the word "elf" because it had been so degraded.[14] He claims that his Elves bear little relation to European varieties; his are men with greatly enhanced aesthetic and creative faculties, greater beauty, nobility, and longer life.[15]

Elves are at the heart of Tolkien's mythology and *The Lord of the Rings,* and at readers' hearts as well. While Sam and Frodo and the fulfillment of their Quest are utmost in our concern, it is often the fate of the Elves, rather than Aragorn's kingship, that touches our emotions and imagination and the loss of their magic in our world that brings such sorrow, even as the tale would seem to end happily.

Traditionally, elves inhabit the realm of Faërie, making occasional forays into the human world, and they are usually disinterested in human affairs. But in Middle-earth they are part of the diverse cultural population. Like other peoples they have their own domains, but they no longer live in a secret, hidden world accessible to man only through magic, and they are central to the events that save the Free Peoples, despite bringing about their own doom of departure.

Tolkien's vision of Faërie is probably best divined in medieval romances like *Sir Launfal, Sir Orfeo,* and *Sir Gawain and the Green Knight,* and his conception of elves may go back even earlier, to Norse and Anglo-Saxon tradition that associates them with secret knowledge and luminosity. The epithet *ælfscienu,* "elf-fair" or "elf-bright," was considered a great compliment to a woman[16] and derives from the light elves of Old Norse mythology, who were fairer than the sun. In "Ides Ælfscyne" ("Elf-Fair Lady"), a poem written in Anglo-Saxon by Tolkien, the appellation is more descriptive than flattering. It is the tale of an elf-maid who seduces a mortal and takes him to her land; disoriented, exiled, and sorrowful, he is returned to his home fifty years later when his family and friends are dead, and he dwindles away, alone.

E<small>UROPEAN</small> B<small>EECH</small>
Fagus sylvatica

them from starvation in the forest. They are Thranduil's folk, and they introduce us to Elves, if we discount the brief visit to Rivendell, where we meet Elrond and learn of his lineage and character but experience little of Elves (except for their singing) and miss the enchanted atmosphere of the place seen in *The Lord of the Rings*.

While not High Elves, Thranduil and his people are presented as complex characters with human attributes in addition to, or perhaps in spite of, their magical powers. They aren't wicked but wary, not cruel but stern, and they have a weakness for good food, wine, and treasure. But their desire for gold is overcome (temporarily) by compassion when they turn aside on their march to Smaug's unguarded hoard to help the dragon's victims at Esgaroth. In the Battle of the Five Armies, they join the Men and Dwarves who also seek the treasure, though some for more charitable reasons than others, but who must forestall their own interests and unite against attacking goblins and wargs. During the War of the Rings, the Wood-elves repulse an attack from Dol Guldur. Elves are fierce warriors, and although Legolas's character in *The Lord of the Rings* is more developed and refined, it is clear that he shares the prowess in battle of his father's folk when necessary.

The Old Forest

Like Mirkwood, the Old Forest has a sinister reputation, although its danger comes from the trees themselves, rather than the forest's inhabitants. The remnant of a vast, ancient wood, the Old Forest borders on Buckland, separated by the Hedge, which the trees once attacked. The hobbits' retaliation of cutting and burning the encroaching trees to contain the forest created enmity between them, and a great distrust and hostility on the part of the trees. That would be frightening enough in a normal forest, but the Old Forest's trees have mobility and intelligence and are directed by a malevolent force, centered in Old Man Willow, who lives on the banks of the Withywindle River (Middle English: *withy*, "willow"; *windle*, "meander").

Frodo, Sam, Merry, and Pippin soon feel the claustrophobic eeriness of the forest as they move through the still, stifling air, cut off from the sky by the forest canopy and crowded by the encroaching trees. The Bonfire Glade, scene of the battle between hobbit and trees, has not recovered, and the flora is dismal; along with nettles and thistles, hemlock and wood parsley grow, not in luxuriant spring green and bloom as in Ithilien, but lanky and faded in autumn decline. Soon lost due to disorientation and diversion by trees, undergrowth and topography, the hobbits realize their journey is being controlled, and the theme of chance and fate is subtly raised, which will be addressed more directly by Bombadil and others throughout *The Lord of the Rings*. There is obviously a force at work that directs them to the Withywindle, precisely the area they wanted to avoid, since it's believed to be the oddest part of the forest. The source may be Old Man Willow or a confluence of energy and will that inhabits the forest, perhaps under his direction; but at a higher level, the Withywindle demonstrates that there are forces against which we are powerless. No matter how hard we struggle to follow our chosen course, as did the hobbits, there are times when we are at the mercy of another influence, which often leads to unexpected results. In the case of the hobbits, their near disaster leads to a fortunate meeting with Tom Bombadil, although he hints that it may have been a greater plan than his, rather than mere chance, that brought them together.[17] While Tom has control over the Great Willow and he and Goldberry have the ability to maintain balance and harmony in nature, they too operate within the Withywindle principle that guides events.

Bombadil tells of the ancient trees' memory of their time as lords, their envy of freely moving beings, and their hatred of the destroyers who invade their home, echoing Tolkien's condemnation of tree killers. Old Man Willow is a characterization of the independent nature and strength of trees, although his is turned to malice. He is the most powerful tree in these woods, and his heartless spirit pervades the Old Forest. His singing is in keeping with the behavior of real willows, whose graceful limbs sway and sigh in the breeze. There are many varieties of willow, of many colors: of those native to Britain are the white willow (*Salix alba*), which grows to eighty feet or more; the sallow (*S. caprea*) or pussy willow; the crack willow (*S. fragilis*); and the osier (*S. viminalis*), the most frequently used in basket making. Treebeard may be a crack willow, so named because the branches break off easily, causing injury to folks standing nearby (rather than swallowing them into cracks in the trunk). Willows love watery locales, and the fallen twigs of the crack willow float along the stream, take root, and line the banks.

Willow was used as a cure for ague and malaria, as well as toothache, headache, and earache. Its efficacy has been proven by the later discovery of salicin in the bark, an element that led to the development of aspirin. Willow wands guarded against thunder and disease and were used by sorcerers and enchanters. Willow had many household uses, particularly the withies, or osiers, the supple shoots that were woven into houses, fences, and baskets, as seen in the whirling House of Rumour in Chaucer's *The House of Fame,* which

Was mad of twigges, falwe, rede,   *yellow, red*
And grene eke, and somme weren white,
Swiche as men to these cages thwite,   *whittle*
Or maken of these panyers,   *bread baskets*
Or elles hottes or dossers,   *baskets*
That for the swough and for the twygges,   *murmuring noise*
This hous was also ful of gygges,   *creaking sounds*
And also ful eke of chirkyges,   *creaking sounds*
And of many other werkynges. (1936–44)

Traditionally, the willow symbolizes the bitterness of grief, because of its acrid taste. For centuries, the willow has been associated with lost love; a cap, sprig, or garland was worn by jilted lovers, a custom that continued into the twentieth century. Shakespeare's Ophelia, driven mad over her father's death and Hamlet's rejection of her love, drowns in a stream where "There is a willow grows askant the brook, / That shows his hoar leaves in the glassy stream" (IV.vii.166–67). An "envious sliver" breaks from the trunk as she tries to hang a garland on the branch, and she is either unable or unwilling to save herself from being dragged to the bottom of the waters by her heavy clothing. Many of us will recall the haunting painting by John Everett Millais, one of the founders of the Pre-Raphaelite Brotherhood, in which a willow hovers over the stream as the witless, singing Ophelia floats away with her woven blooms.

The willow tree's aura of beauty, utility, healing, danger, history, sorrow, grief, and magic may surround Old Man Willow, if only by virtue of his species, but it does not explain Tolkien's choice of the tree for such a vicious character, especially considering his beloved childhood climbing tree. Perhaps the Great Willow's rancor is motivated by the desire to gain retribution for the wanton destruction of Tolkien's willow and many trees like it and others in the Old Forest, their hearts hardened by endless years of injury and lost dignity.

Lothlórien

We visited Lothlórien briefly during our tour of Middle-earth, and we will once again pass through quickly, because the atmosphere of Lórien cannot be captured by analysis but only through personal experience. It is a world apart, unlike other forests of Middle-earth; like other woods, it is ancient and full of memories, but in Lothlórien the past seems to live in the present, defying the sense of history so carefully constructed for the rest of Middle-earth. Time, too, passes at a different rate, although the seasons appear to accord with those outside, to which the unique flora of Lórien responds. Unlike trees in other forests, the *mallorns* have no independent personality or character; although palpably alive, they serve to house the Elves. Caras Galadon resembles a walled medieval city, and it is tempting to envision a great center built of magnificent towerlike trees as Tolkien's ideal urban environment.[18]

Unlike Ithilien, where the atmosphere derives greatly from the flora, the source of Lórien's aura, beauty, and mystery is its inhabitants. Unlike in Fangorn, where the danger comes from the trees, peril in Lórien comes from the Elves who rule and guard it, although they react to the threat presented by each individual. While other forests are forbidding but accessible, Lórien is hidden and forbidden; it is protected by Galadriel from the evil of Sauron that invaded Mirkwood, and there are none of the spots of Morgoth's Darkness that lurk in the Old Forest and Fangorn. And unlike the other forests of Middle-earth, Lothlórien does not flourish after the Third Age and the passing of the Elves. Already faded from the Land of the Valley of Singing Gold to the Dreamflower, Lórien's spring and summer have passed, never to be seen again except, as Galadriel says, in memory; in her lament, she foresees that for Lórien "The Winter comes, the bare and leafless Day; / The leaves are falling in the stream, the River flows away."[19] But, as Legolas tells his companions in order to ease their sorrow when leaving Lothlórien, their memories of the place will always remain fresh and clear, which is true for the travelers, readers, and author.

Fangorn Forest

The most impressive trees or, more properly, treelike creatures, are the Ents, among the most naturally powerful and dangerous beings on Middle-earth. They, like many other characters and events, were not consciously created; Tolkien says in Letter 163 that Treebeard's chapter was written much as it stands, almost as if someone else wrote it. However, he is very clear on the source of his inspiration: the Anglo-Saxon poem "The Wanderer" (circa tenth century).[20] The name "Ent," or "giant," comes from a line of this elegiac tale of a man alone on the sea, friendless after the death of his lord. As he reflects on the transience of worldly wealth and goods, he remembers happy days in the mead halls that now decay, and the comradeship of warriors now fallen and silent. The "mouldering ruins" of ancient "eald enta geweorc idlu stondon" ("giant-built structures [that] stand empty of life") lead him to ask,

Where now is the warrior? Where is the war horse?
Bestowal of treasure, and sharing of feast?
Alas! the bright ale-cup, the byrny-clad warrior,
The prince in his splendor—those days are long sped
In the night of the past, as if they never had been! (84–88)

The lament of the fleeting days of glory is expressed in the *ubi sunt* ("where are") motif, the formula derived from the opening words of a type of medieval Latin poem taken up in Old English poetry. In keeping with the Anglo-Saxon nature of Rohan culture, Tolkien employs the form for the Song of the Rohirrim that Aragorn chants as the travelers pass the burial mounds of past kings, covered with *Simbelmynë*, or Evermind:

Where now the horse and rider? Where is the horn that was
    blowing?
Where is the helm and the hauberk, and the bright hair flowing? . . .
They have passed like rain on the mountain, like a wind in the
    meadow;
The days have gone down in the West behind the hills into
    shadow.[21]

The Ents' speech reflects their complex, carefully deliberate, and comparatively leisurely thought process, although Entish is not their only language. They prefer Quenya and Sindarin and often combine ancient Elvish words in an Entish manner into musical, descriptive linkages.[22] Despite the Ents' long relationship with the Elves, Treebeard is not among the Wise and there are many things that he does not understand, including, by his own admission, the process by which Ents become trees and vice versa. Rather, he possesses deep memory and knowledge of earth, wood, and, according to mythic allusion, stone.

Fangorn, "The Ent," or Treebeard in Westron, is the oldest of three remaining Ents who lived in the Great Wood before the Darkness of Morgoth entered and sundered the forest that covered Middle-earth during the First Age. He is a rather mysterious character, and even Tolkien isn't sure of Treebeard's origin or full history. Gandalf's description of Treebeard as the oldest living being walking on Middle-earth must be accurate, since his knowledge in such matters is unfailing (while Treebeard's knowledge of wizards is quite meager). The lore, however, is a bit muddled. In Gandalf's riddle about the Ents' power, we learn that "Ere iron was found or tree was hewn, / When young was mountain under moon; / Ere ring was made, or wrought was woe, / It walked the forests long ago,"[23] and Tolkien informs us that Ents are the most ancient creatures living in the Third Age. Yet Treebeard names Elves as the eldest, coming before Ents in the Old Lists, while Celeborn addresses the Ent as "eldest," an appellation Tom Bombadil applies to himself and who is also named "oldest and fatherless" by Elrond. The apparent puzzle results from the different types of beings that inhabit Middle-earth, which are not always easy to categorize. Bombadil and Treebeard can both be "eldest" since Tom is apart from, and antecedent to, the other living creatures, peoples, flora, fauna, and elements, while Treebeard was first to walk through the young woods, although many of the trees in Fangorn are older than he. The Eldars' essence is far beyond the realm of Middle-earth, and although they are counted as one of the Free Peoples, their history cannot be measured with that of other inhabitants of Middle-earth.

Treebeard remembers the time when Elves taught trees to speak and when they fled at Morgoth's arrival. He tells how Darkness remained in parts of the different woods and that trees have long memories, although not all have bad hearts like Old Man Willow; in fact, he once knew some very sweet willows.[24] But there is danger in every forest, according to its nature. Celeborn warned against Fangorn, and Treebeard would do the same of Lórien, though each possesses its own mysterious peril and pleasure. In Fangorn, there are places of green, glistening beauty, as well as pockets of blackness away from which the Ents guide strangers, while they keep a watchful shepherd's eye over all.

These treeherders are slow to be roused but deliberate and thorough in their devastation of Orthanc when enraged. Like Tom Bombadil, Treebeard is aware of events outside of his own realm but is little motivated to participate; the Ents' involvement in the defeat of Saruman is driven as much out of self-protection due to the destruction of their home and kin as concern for the greater cause. Yet their desire for self-preservation cannot elude the adverse effects of self-interest, which results in the decline of their species.

There has been critical discussion of Tolkien's literary treatment of women and male/female relationships, and the sad tale of the Ents and Entwives is a strong refutation of charges that Tolkien had little understanding in that area. While the male herders represent an uncontrolling love of nature, which is a reflection of Bombadil's mastery rather than ownership and the difference between botany and agriculture, the Entwives exercise domination over their gardens. Ents and Entwives also present a realistic counter to the idealistic harmony of thought and action between Tom Bombadil and Goldberry. The separation of Ents and their wives results from a lack of shared goals and from their failure to understand or value each other's beliefs and desires. Without compromise, relationships will founder and paths will separate. Neither their ancient wisdom nor the need to perpetuate their dwindling race can save the Ents from "human" frailty in marital relationships.

But the Ents are capable of collaboration and organization, as seen in the Entmoot (held at Derndingle: ME *dern*, "secret," "hidden"; *dingle* ME derivation, "deep wooded valley or dell") and their attack on Isengard. As with his naming of the Ents, Tolkien explains the inspiration for their march in one of his letters.[25] He recalls being disgusted as a schoolboy by the treatment of trees in *Macbeth;* the "coming of the Great Birnam wood to high Dunsinane" is derailed by humans, and Tolkien wanted to give trees the opportunity to really march. (Tolkien seems to have had a general antipathy for Shakespeare.) Macbeth relies on the prophesy that he "shall never vanquish'd be until / Great Birnam wood to high Dunsinane hill / Shall come against him (IV.i.92–94), since trees can't walk. However, Malcolm orders his soldiers when passing through the wood as they advance against Macbeth at Dunsinane to cut and carry a bough, using the "leavy screens" to conceal their approach. Macbeth's men are astonished to see a forest move, as is Macbeth to find that the prognostication of a fiend could fail. The sudden appearance of a forest is reenacted in the Huorns' traveling woods, and those trees are at least as dangerous as Malcolm's soldiers and far more mysterious and terrifying. Both Macbeth, who felt protected by supernatural prophecy, and Saruman, who counted on his wizardly powers,

ROWAN TREE
Sorbus aucuparia

are overcome, and Tolkien makes sure that the trees get their revenge against the "Tree-killer" and his Orcs personally.

Before we leave Fangorn Forest, there is one more tree that deserves attention: the rowan. We are introduced to its beauty by Merry and Pippin's companion Bregalad, whose name in Common Speech, Quickbeam, is one of the names by which the rowan has been known for centuries. Quickbeam's house is surrounded by rowan trees, and he tells the hobbits of rowans he once loved, now destroyed by Orcs.[26] His lamenting description of the trees' bright berries and their attractiveness to birds recalls a late medieval Irish poem:

> Glen of the rowan trees with scarlet berries,
> With fruit praised by every flock of birds,
> A slumbrous paradise for any badger
> In their quiet burrows with their young.[27]

In addition to its beauty, the rowan has been prized for its protective powers against evil forces and beings, including witches and fairies, who may steal or curdle milk or enchant fires. Rowan can release a captive from within a fairy circle and keep the dead from rising; it can also avert or cure sickness caused by elf-shot arrows that inflict sudden pain and illnesses like arthritis and rheumatism.[28] Perhaps most importantly, rowan was, and is, believed to protect the home from evil spirits and is planted near the house, like those that surround the mossy stone and green turves of Quickbeam's Ent-house. It seems doubtful that the resemblance of that setting to the scene of Boromir's attack on Frodo is coincidental. There, too, a flat stone sits on the grass amidst rowan trees, an environment in which the hobbit might find some protection from the hostility he senses when Boromir enters the area. However, the rowan's power to combat evil cannot protect Boromir from the Ring's influence, and Frodo is able to perceive the man's intent and parry his assault until Boromir succumbs completely to the temptation of the Ring, which Frodo must then use to escape.

The Power of Trees and Nature

Trees have been central to man's material life from early history as a chief source of housing, household furnishings and implements, tools, food, and many other practical uses, as well as having symbolic and metaphysical importance. In Old English, *treow* had multiple meanings: tree; truth, fidelity, trust, and belief; pledge, agreement; and favor, kindness. Words with a double meaning representing "tree" and "trust" are found in several other languages, based on the dependability and permanence of trees.[29]

In an obliquely related manner, runes possessed dual properties, both practical and representational. Runology is extremely complex, but (overly) simplistically described, runic letters combine both sound, for use in an alphabetic system, and symbol. Tolkien created his own system, although it appears to have been used mainly for written communication only. In the "Old English Rune Poem,"* several characters are associated with

---

* Recorded in George Hickes's *Linguarum Veterum Septentrionalium Thesaurus* (1705) from a lost original possibly dated to the ninth century or later. Pollington, *Runes* 45.

trees; the letter is accompanied by a verse, which begins with the sound of the character, its name, and then its association. For example:

ᚪ "āc" (OE "a") means oak, or ship made of oak. The oak was used as ship-building material, for leather tanning, in houses, churches, and cathedrals, and the acorns were fed to swine. Thus, the

> Oak is for the sons of men on earth
> a feeder of flesh, often travels
> over gannet's bath, the ocean tests
> whether the oak keeps good faith.[30]

ᛇ "ēoh" (OE "eo") (not to be confused with "eoh," warhorse) is the yew tree, whose hard wood was used for bows. The tree is exceptionally long-lived, and its leaves are poisonous, leading to an association with life and death. In medieval times, the tree was planted near the home, often near gables and chimneys, for protection from the wind. It was also traditionally planted in churchyards, although the reasons for the custom are still debated. In later years, it acquired a more negative image than presented in the "Old English Rune Poem":

> Yew is an unsmooth tree outside
> hard, earthfast, fire's keeper
> underpinned with roots, a joy in the homeland.[31]

The honoring of the uses, properties, and energies of trees and plants and the extension of their strength into the metaphysical realm, which has been inseparable from the physical world since the earliest cultures, are expressed in many types of traditions and lore, such as runes and leech-craft. The attribution of medicinal and protective properties to plant life is very ancient, and although we may think of it as "prescientific," much continues to the current time. While some, like salicin in the willow bark, has been proven efficacious, most are not demonstrable in clinical or rational terms. But the premise on which the lore is founded, that there is power in nature and, specifically, flora, symbolizes our hope and belief that there are forces beyond those of human construct and understanding.

Power, and its different uses and manifestations, is a central motif in *The Lord of the Rings,* although Tolkien considers it only a driving force

E N G L I S H   O A K
Quercus robur

of other more central themes, particularly mortality and immortality. It is most obvious as the desire for dominion and the countering desire for freedom, wielded by both natural and supernatural forces and beings. Tolkien's attention to the power of nature is often neglected by critics, especially his botany, excepting perhaps the strength and character of the Ents and Old Man Willow. But as we have seen, almost every plant in *The Lord of the Rings* carries lore, symbolism, and cultural connotations that express belief in nature's power and wisdom. Plants have much to offer man, if he listens. In the Finnish folk epic the *Kalevala*, which was another of Tolkien's inspirations for language and the *Silmarillion* mythology, the poet tells of the ways in which he gathered and stored his knowledge:

> There are many other legends;
> Songs I learned of magic import;
> Some beside the pathway gathered;
> Others broken from the heather;
> Others wrested from the bushes;

Others taken from the saplings,
Gathered from the springing verdure,
Or collected from the by-ways
As I passed along as herd-boy.
(Runo I:51–59)

We have seen repeatedly and clearly that Tolkien honored nature over machine and perceived the perils of modernization. So far, we have focused on his treatment of nature, so it is fitting to take a look at its nemesis. Our study of botany has been based to a great extent in the medieval atmosphere of both Middle-earth and Tolkien's literary and philosophical orientation, as well as contemporary movements that resonate with his love of nature and simplicity over technology and industrialization. This approach is supported by many of Tolkien's letters and is most dramatically evidenced in *The Lord of the Rings,* although there is a hint in *The Hobbit.* Smoke and vapor pour out of the front door to Smaug's cave, and the rocky hills, black water, and single stunted, leafless tree in Tolkien's drawing of the scene may be a "metaphor for the industrial landscape" he detested.[32]

Middle-earth is set in a prescientific, preindustrial age, but it is as complex and sophisticated as the worlds of *Beowulf* and *Sir Gawain and the Green Knight* and their political, ideological, economic, and cultural realities. We must therefore consider the place of technology in Middle-earth, as well as in Tolkien's England. We think of "modern" technology, often without an extensive knowledge of the "premodern" technology that is implied by the term. There are numerous excellent histories of medieval and premodern technology based on documents, archaeology, and material evidence, particularly for agrarian societies like that of the Shire.[33] Although the upper limits of machinery in the Shire are the forge-bellows, water-mill, and hand-loom, we can observe the hobbits' successful agricultural technology in their crop production and quality, their healthy economy, comfortable lifestyle, and leisure time. In his prologue Tolkien mentions a wide range of economic status between hobbits, but "poorest" appears to be a relative term and poverty is not seen in the Shire.

Again, we recall the Arts and Crafts movement's reaction to nineteenth-century factory mechanization and mass production: a return to pre–industrial age technology that brought workers back into connection with their product and craft, engendered pride in workmanship, and served individual and community. In *The Lord of the Rings*, the rumblings of Mt. Doom are likened to throbbing engines, and the technology of Sauron and Saruman, who Treebeard describes as having a "mind of metal and wheels,"[34] is used for war machinery, enslavement, destruction, and domination. It mirrors industrial-age technology, especially in large centers like Birmingham, where Tolkien lived much of his life; smoke and noxious fumes rise from furnaces and fires through shafts from tunnels and caves beneath Isengard where smithies and iron wheels thud and revolve continuously. Sharkey's Mill in the Shire is the perfect metaphor for Industrial Revolution ugliness and dehumanization. The building that replaces the family-operated Sandyman's mill has a tall chimney (the sort Tolkien sarcastically extols as being more alive and real than an elm tree in "On Fairy-stories"[35]); it is filled with wheels and "outlandish contraptions"[36] that hammer incessantly but are no longer used for grinding corn, and black smoke spews from its chimney. The new mill and Shirriff-houses are constructed of ugly, poorly laid brick, and when those hated structures are destroyed, the bricks are used to repair hobbit homes to their former snugness and to line new holes.

Here we encounter a situation as perplexing as Tolkien's tree choice for Old Man Willow: the resemblance between Sarehole Mill and Sharkey's. Putting together Carpenter's description and information published by Birmingham,[37] Sarehole Mill is a brick building with a tall chimney, water wheel, and steam engine for use when water power is low; inside there are leather belts, pulleys, shafts, and other milling machinery. Originally a corn mill, in Tolkien's time it ground bones for manure. Tolkien's fond memories of the area and its basis for Hobbiton are well known (including mushroom stealing), so the similarity between the two mills is puzzling.

The brick building that so saddens the hobbits is nearer to an industrial structure than a village mill, as foreseen by Sam in Galadriel's mirror. Its material is the red brick of Dickens's Coketown, where factories' steam engines, deep furnaces, and towering chimneys pour out endless streams of smoke and ash, where "Nature was as strongly bricked out as killing airs and gases were bricked in."[38] Brick has been used since medieval times, and we learn in the Prologue that some hobbit dwellings are constructed of brick, as well as wood and stone, and that brick is preferred by millers, cartwrights, and other workmen. Bricks were favored in the Arts and Crafts style for garden paths and walls; they were the main material for Morris's magnificent home, the Red House. But they were prized as products of local origin and craftsmanship and used as design elements, quite unlike the red bricks of the industrial age, mass-produced blocks used for grim institutional structures like Sharkey's Mill.

Sarehole Mill was originally built in the mid-sixteenth century and has been rebuilt many times, the current buildings dating to the early nineteenth century and, it may be imagined, architecturally more graceful than Sharkey's crude structure. It was a corn mill for three centuries, and it was also used for button making in the eighteenth century. During the Industrial Revolution it was used for blade grinding and metal rolling, then bone grinding. Despite Tolkien's happy childhood experiences, as an adult he may have envisioned the mill as it was originally, an operation that served the community rather than industry, and he freed it of all vestiges of modern or misused technology through the eradication of Sharkey's Mill.

The odd similarities between Sarehole and ravaged Hobbiton extend beyond the mills. The sandpit near the Sarehole Mill that served the Tolkien boys as a playground is seen in the sand quarry that replaces destroyed Bagshot Row, and the row of houses on Gracewell recalls the new row of houses built by Sharkey (Saruman). During a visit to Sarehole in 1933, recorded in his diary, Tolkien found his childhood home engulfed in a "sea of new red-brick." The village had become a suburb of Birmingham, and he found the changes "violent and peculiarly hideous,"[39] although the process had begun when Tolkien lived there; even then, Sarehole was being encroached upon in order to provide accommodations for Birmingham's expanding labor force. The family's semidetached brick cottage and its row had actually been built only a few years before they moved there in 1896, the same year that Morris advised Londoners in *The Earthly Paradise* to "Forget the snorting steam engine and piston stroke, / Forget the spreading of the hideous town" and to return to an earlier time of clear skies and green gardens.[40] From the reader's perspective, Tolkien's revisited Sarehole, childhood Sarehole, and Sharkey's Hobbiton are merged, restored, and protected from industrial "progress."

The technology that drives Saruman's and Sauron's desires for power over nature and Man is most cursed for the destruction of flora, especially trees. The orchards of Isengard are replaced by stone and metal, trees in Fangorn are felled to fuel the fires of Orthanc or sometimes simply out of malice, and Mordor is a barren wasteland, pocked with pits and pools of poisonous debris. The defilement of the Shire by Saruman is heartbreaking: homes and gardens deserted (there are few sadder sights than a garden that has been let die) or replaced by gravel pits and quarries, water polluted, avenues of trees destroyed, hedgerows broken, and, perhaps most grievous of all, the Party Tree chopped down and left dead in the field. But once rid of Saruman and his influence, the hobbits quickly begin the work of restoration, starting with new homes for the displaced Bagshot Row residents (renamed New Row) and the replacement of the sandpit with a sheltered garden.

CHAPTER 5

RESTORATION AND RECOVERY

ecovery from the damage caused by the Enemy in the Shire and all of Middle-earth starts almost immediately after his defeat and the restoration of the kingship and its line, the geographic and political center of which is Minas Tirith: the Tower of the Guard, capital of Anárien, and chief city of Gondor. One of the cities created by the exiled Númenóreans when they arrived in Middle-earth and established the realms of Arnor and Gondor, it was built by Elendil's younger son, Anárion, and named Minas Anor, the Tower of the Rising Sun. His older brother, Isildur, built Minas Ithil, the Tower of the Rising Moon, which was taken by Sauron and became Minas Morgul. Minas Anor survived destruction or seizure during the War of the Last Alliance; it was renamed Minas Tirith, and the White Tower, site of the king's hall and throne, was constructed on the citadel.

Built into the side of a hill, Minas Tirith, like many of Tolkien's habitations, seems part of the earth. It takes advantage of a lofty rock bastion that bifurcates the city and provides a vantage point as part of the extraordinary defense system that protects the king's abode. The city climbs the hill within seven circles of fortified walls, each with gates offset from the other levels. Once a thriving place, its houses, halls, and courts are mostly deserted, both from the city's waning glory and the evacuation of women, children, and the aged due to the impending war. There is an outer wall, the Rammas Echor, and between that defense and the city lies the Pelennor, with its fertile fields, townlands inhabited by herdsmen and husbandmen, and their homesteads, orchards, terraces, kilns, granaries, and livestock areas. Now, however, no animals can be seen, and the many roads that cross the fields are crowded with wagons and traffic related to wartime preparations. Several times in *The Lord of the Rings,* Tolkien gives the human face of battle in its effects on the folk: families separated, husbands and sons lost. The destruction of countryside when homes, barns, fields, and trees are burned is seen during the Battle of the Pelennor, and mourned by Théoden earlier in the rich Westfold Vale of his people during the attack on Helm's Deep.

Tolkien's description of Minas Tirith is detailed so that the city can be visualized and entered imaginatively for a sense of familiarity, as can other locales in which the characters and readers spend time. On the larger scale, however, things become more vague, both geographically and politically. While we are given an intricate history of "The Ordering of the Shire" and its governance in the prologue, the rest of Middle-earth receives no concentrated attention. Unless we cull the appendices and the *Silmarillion* and string together references sprinkled throughout *The Lord of the Rings* text, which often requires some searching, we are left with an impression of vast space comprised of territories and lands often described through general geographical references.

Although some readers found this frustrating and Tolkien was pressed for more concrete facts after the first two books, the feeling of expansive, diffuse space allows the reader an unlimited range of imaginative exploration that extends the boundaries of depth and scope. Despite Tolkien's absorption in the continuing history, which, like Niggle's Tree, always begged additions, he suggested that the appendices and their ponderous information might detract from the "unexplained vistas" that are "part of the literary effect"[1] and could properly be neglected by readers who wish to experience the tale as it stands, without apocryphal references. However, the hazy nature of Aragorn's kingdom is unfortunate for our botanical tour, since several areas sound as though they would have much to offer, like Lossarnach, where the fields and woods are filled with flowers in spring, and lush Lebennin, which is so fair that Tolkien invented blooms, "the golden bells of *mallos* and *alfirin*" that remain in Legolas's memory.[2]

But we can see Minas Tirith fairly well. In Tolkien's artwork, it resembles a walled medieval town, and indeed it is typical with its towers, battlements, and banners. However, as Legolas notes, it is lacking one usual feature: gardens. While historicizing Minas Tirith would detract from its romantic and epic qualities, it is true that gardens were common in almost every kind of medieval dwelling environment, from peasant cottages to monasteries, manor houses, castles, and urban centers, whether for culinary, medicinal, pleasure, or revenue-generating purposes. Large cities usually were surrounded by suburban fields like those in the Pelennor, reflecting the close relationship between urban and agricultural life, but they would also have gardens within the walls. In Minas Tirith, the only garden we see is next to the Houses of Healing, and it appears to be a pleasure park with grass and trees; it might be imagined that some medicinal herbs would be grown there also, although many, like *athelas,* would be gathered from their natural habitats.

That garden is the site of the happy reunion of Pippin, Merry, Legolas, and Gimli, who share stories of their experiences (and unite several narrative strands) while they were in separate realms. It is also where Faramir and Éowyn meet and come to know each other, walking, talking, and sometimes sitting in silence. The placement of such a park near the Houses of Healing demonstrates a belief in the restorative quality of a natural setting where patients and others in need of recovery can feel the warmth of the sun, benefit from quiet contemplation, and, as here, come to know themselves and others with a cleared vision. After the war, as Legolas promised, there are many fountains, trees, and gardens planted in Minas Tirith, and birdsong fills the air along with children's laughter.

The White Tower and the Court of the Fountain are located on the uppermost level of Minas Tirith, the citadel; the fountain is surrounded by grass, and in the center is the dead White Tree of Gondor, token of the house of Elendil and Aragorn's kingship. Inside the great Tower Hall, the image of the Tree in flower is carved on the wall behind the empty throne that awaits the return of the king. It is also emblazoned on the guards' livery and gleams on Aragorn's banner, encircled by seven stars and a crown, wrought by Arwen in gems and *mithril*. The White Tree of Gondor has a very long and complex history, and the myth may well have been inspired by a tale in the *Kalevala* of the theft of the sun and moon from the fir and birch trees in which they were settled, which Tolkien illustrated in *The Land of Pohja* in 1914.[3]

The Tree's lineage begins in Valinor with Telperion, one of the Two Trees of the Valar, images of which are seen on Durin's Doors to Moria. Another tree was created in Telperion's image, and its sapling appeared in Númenor as Nimloth, a tree with dark, silver-lined foliage and white flowers that gave fragrance in the evening. Sauron hewed and burned Nimloth, but Isildur had stolen a fruit from the Tree, which was planted and sprouted, so that the line continued in secret. He guarded the sapling, which he brought to Middle-earth when the Númenóreans were exiled, and planted it in Minas Ithil in memory of the Tree's parentage in the land of the Valar. Again, Sauron destroyed the Tree, and again Isildur saved a seedling and planted it in Minas Anor in memory of his brother, Anárion, who fell during the War of the Last Alliance. The Tree died during the Great Plague, and its replacement also died and no new sapling could be found; the dead Tree stood as the sign of the failing of the kingship and the decline of Gondor's strength.

The Withered Tree's barrenness represents the need for the final, and perhaps most important, event of Aragorn's long journey: marriage to Arwen and the continuation of his line to rule the Reunited Kingdom of Arnor and Gondor. Aragorn's love for Arwen Evenstar and the depth of their relationship is portrayed in fleeting but intensely revealing passages and is at the center of his efforts to reclaim the kingship. Hope is renewed and desire fulfilled when Gandalf finds a sapling of the White Tree, which is planted in place of the old and flourishes in the Court of the Fountain. Tolkien tells of hearing rhyme lores, the meaning of which became apparent to him later; one was "seven stars and seven stones and one white tree."[4] One of his unused dust jacket designs for *The Return of the King* features Elendil's monogram; the emblem of his line, the Seven Stars; the empty throne awaiting Aragorn; the winged crown of Gondor; the green gem of King Elessar; and the White Tree with seven flowers.[5]

As destruction of plant life is one of the most heinous manifestations of Sauron's force, the restoration of flora is one of the most visible symbols of the victory over his power and the renewal of the reign of Elendil's line and Gondor's glory, which spread throughout the Reunited Kingdom. Several of Middle-earth's forests suffered harm during Sauron's quest for dominion, some peripherally as he strengthened his forces and operations, and others directly during the War. But as we have seen, most of the forests thrive after the removal of the Enemy's influence. The Old Forest, the least directly contaminated by his evil, likely remains the same, while Mirkwood is home to Thranduil's Elven folk, and the Beornings and Woodmen. Isengard is restored to its verdant condition, renamed the Treegarth of Orthanc by Treebeard. Fangorn Forest is expanded by the land granted to the Ents by Aragorn, although the New Age will not bring a reconciliation with the Entwives. Ithilien's vestiges of greatness are invigorated and surpassed. Only Lórien and East Lórien (southern Mirkwood) do not become part of the Age of Man, their Elven spirit doomed with the end of the Third Age.

The Fourth Age is brought to pass by many peoples of lofty and ancient lineage, whose cultures and lands recall past grandeur that will be renewed under King Elessar's rule. But at the heart of the Quest are the humble hobbits and their home, which has been the touchstone throughout the tale for them and the reader. So it is in the Shire that the most vigorous and consoling restoration takes place. The Shire was violated in many ways, and recovery is needed to rebuild community relationships that were splintered during Saruman's occupation, to cope with the effects of hostile action and violent death in the hobbits' usually peaceful and protected homeland, and to return to normalcy after chaos and fear. And the members of the Fellowship must adjust to life in their beloved but insular home after their extraordinary adventures.

Thanks to the indomitable, rustic hobbit spirit, recovery begins quickly and soon surpasses expectations or hopes. Thanks, too, to Sam's tireless work, aided by Galadriel's parting gift, the Shire is soon graced again with many trees; the most marvelous, of course, is the *mallorn* that replaces the felled tree at the center of the Party Field, the site and symbol of communal life and friendship. Crops are plentiful, as are children, and maid-children continue to be given floral names, including four of Sam and Rosie's: Rose, Primrose, Daisy, and Elanor the Fair.

The concepts of renewal and recovery imply loss and change; not all losses can be restored, and some things can never be the same. Nor should they be. Some wounds, like Frodo's, can never be fully healed, and we all bear marks, for good or ill, from our experiences. *The Lord of the Rings* is the story of the passage from one age to another, and transition means change. The magic of Elves and Wizards is lost to Middle-earth, though it will pass into the New Age as a memory of enchantment, and the reuniting of Elendil's kingdom will bring new and renewed alliances and restored strength and dignity.

The arrival of the Fourth Age brings change, recovery, and renewal to the characters in *The Lord of the Rings,* but Tolkien felt that recovery is also important for the reader. In "On Fairy-stories" he defines recovery as the gaining of a renewed view of things that have become stale or taken for granted through familiarity. Successful sub-creation can bring a refreshed vision, an objectivity to enhance appreciation, enjoyment, and understanding.[6] Of course, *The Lord of the Rings* cannot become commonplace, regardless of how often we read it. But hopefully an awareness of its plant life will offer a new perspective for future visits to Middle-earth.

APPENDIX A

ABOUT PLANT LORE

This is intended as a (very) basic primer for readers who are unfamiliar with plant lore. There are many fine sources available for those who would like to learn more, some of which are listed in the bibliography and are the source of the information presented here.[1]

Today, the use of plants for treating illness and maintaining health is considered "alternative" medicine and is just beginning to make inroads into established medical practice. To many, it stands on the fringe of science and tradition. Yet for centuries plants and other natural substances were at the core of healing, part of cosmological phenomena and rhythms. Rituals, charms, and spells developed around the use of natural materials at a time when medicine and magic were intermingled. Knowledge was discovered through observation and trial and error and transmitted through both learned writings and folklore, representing the different strains of healing at the professional and native levels. Both were involved in the identification of plants and herbs and their properties and uses.

Ancient and classical cultures investigated the natural sciences, and many Greek and Latin writings remained influential for centuries. Herbal treatises addressed medical remedies made from "simples," plants with healing properties, though they were far from what we now consider scientific and accurate. Some were illustrated, although usually copied from other texts rather than drawn from observation, so that the representations often suffered in the process. Not until the fourteenth and fifteenth centuries did herbals contain illustrations drawn from nature, particularly by the Italians. The uses of herbals are difficult to determine; some may have been used for teaching, as working manuals by practitioners, in monastic infirmaries, or possibly collected as antiquaries.[2] While there is a common perception that healing was the province of the monasteries, there is evidence of lay physicians,[3] and Collins dispels the idea of a clerical monopoly on the production of herbals.[4]

Notable among the classics are the first-century Greek *De Materia Medica* of Pedanius Dioscorides and the fourth-century Latin *Herbarium* of Apuleius Platonicus, whose works in compilations with others were circulated, translated, and copied throughout the Middle Ages, including into English vernacular. There are four extant copies of Old English translations of Apuleius's *Herbarium,* which gives information on 159 plants and may have served practicing physicians. There are a sizable number of Old English medical texts, which blend classical sources with folk custom and Christian belief. A particularly good example, although full of errors and inconsistencies, is the tenth-century *Lacnunga,* which gives recipes, rituals, and prayers, seemingly randomly collected into a personal "commonplace" book by a nonspecialist:[5]

Against a scabby body: dig up sorrel and yellodwort, pulling up lengthways; pound them all well: boil in butter, add a little salt; that will be a good salve against a scabby body; wash the man with it hot and smear him with the salve.[6]

Blessing of the ointments. God, almighty father, and Jesus Christ, son of God, I ask that you will stoop to send your blessing and heavenly medicine and godly protection over this ointment so that it may produce health and cure against all the bodies' diseases or of its parts, whether inside or outside, for all using that ointment.[7]

The compilation known as Bald's *Leechbooks* (c. 950) is probably the oldest surviving complete medical work in Old English, and Book 3 is possibly the most reflective of early English medical practice.[8] Book 3 is stronger in folkloric elements than the other two books in the compendium and includes ritual and prayer amongst the curative recipes:

A light drink for a frenzy: lupin, bishopwort, elfthon, elecampane, cropleek, hindhealth, radish, burdock; take these plants when day and night divide, sing the litany first in church, and the 'credo,' and 'pater noster,' go while singing to the plants, go round them thrice, before you take them and go back to the church and sing twelve masses over the plants when you have steeped them.[9]

Rituals and charms were used in gathering and preparing plants and materials in order to channel and direct their powers and were a spoken, chanted, sung, or written verse act performed in a sacred language.[10] Not all herbals contained charms but were of the treatise type that encompassed plant names, lists of synonyms, characteristics, distribution and habitat, earlier authors' observations, methods of gathering and preparation, recipes, curative uses, and contraindications.[11]

Herbals, encyclopedias, lists, and treatises on plants continued to be compiled, translated, and copied throughout Europe, and texts in vernacular English moved into the age of printing in 1525 with the anonymous *Bancke's Herbal* (named after the publisher) and toward science. William Turner's *A New Herball* (1551–68) was the first scientific study of plants and marked the "beginning of the science of botany in England,"[12] and John Gerard's *The Herball or General Historie of Plants* (1597) remains "a bible to English herbalists."[13]

If we jump ahead to the seventeenth century, we see the enduring influence of the classical and medieval herbals. Astrological physician Nicholas Culpeper's *Complete Herbal and English Physician,* written in 1652, was extremely popular; forty-five editions were produced before the end of the eighteenth century.[14] It was also reprinted in the early nineteenth century as what we now know as modern medicine was developing. In the preface to that edition, Culpeper is extolled for making knowledge about natural remedies and materials available to the common man, in reaction to those contemporary practitioners who lack compassion and are motivated solely by fees. It explains that Culpeper's approach was at odds with that of other physicians of his day and that he, too, had found practitioners governed by avarice rather than the desire to heal.

In his *Complete Herbal,* Culpeper presents plants' names, description, times of growth and harvest, astrological governance, essential qualities (hot, cold, moist, etc.), habitat, virtues, properties, uses, and recipes. He subscribed to the ancient Doctrine of Signatures, which held that the physical appearance of a plant gives clues to its use through similarity to the body part(s) it treats; for example, the roots of the lesser celandine look like hemorrhoids, and the plant (still known as pilewort) was thus used to cure the condition. He was well read in the classical and medieval herbals and natural science studies, from which he drew freely, and his repository of knowledge and lore is still valuable to researchers. A random, precursory comparison between Culpeper's work and the *Old English Herbarium* reveals shared knowledge about the healing properties of some plants and herbs, although many differ and/or have been expanded upon. For example, both recommend saxifrage as a diuretic and cure for "gravel," or bladder stones; marjoram for clearing chest diseases that cause cough and hinder breathing, and for liver illnesses; fennel for bladder pain and stones, and shortness of breath, wheezing, and coughing; chervil for stomach pain; celandine for soreness and dimness of the eyes, and for "kernels" (swellings); and rue for nosebleeds, dimness of eyesight, and stomach pains. At the same time, the seventeenth century also saw Harvey's demonstration of the circulation system, and the movement toward scientific medicine started creeping forward until plants and herbs were eventually marginalized. Ironically, many modern drugs were originally derived from plant materials and then synthesized.

But our interest is in plant lore, of which healing is an aspect, rather than medical science, so we are going to pursue ethnopharmaceuticals and ethnobotany and follow the path of the folk. While much plant and healing lore was captured in herbal treatises, it also existed as native custom alongside and beyond written record. In England, the focus of our study, efforts to collect and record folk plant and herb lore have waxed and waned, and, as with the herbals, much of the information presented in early publications came from previous sources, including non-British. Starting in the seventeenth century, interest was taken in local flora; plant names, customs, and uses vary regionally, and Britain's first county flora was published in 1660. Other compilations of local plant life followed later, though only a few were based on personal observation rather than on other works. The nineteenth century saw a proliferation of plant folklore studies, though not all contained authenticated material, and plant lore was included in some broader folkloric studies.

Unlike Ireland, Wales, and Scotland, which have formed official organizations and institutions for plant and folklore studies as part of national pride, England has "not considered it necessary to gather their folklore and use it to establish an identity" due to their national dominance.[15] So, with a few exceptions, studies have been conducted sporadically and informally by individuals and local folklore societies. However, there has been an increase in interest and publications since the late twentieth century. Regardless of its status as a study subject or its relationship to medical science, plant lore persists. Using Vickery's *Dictionary,* which presents samplings of modern folk belief from locations throughout Britain, we see that plants still serve curative and utilitarian purposes as in medieval times, though somewhat updated:

> You choose good green ivy leaves, wash them and dry them; boil in fresh lard enough leaves to turn the lard a rich green colour—they crisp up in boiling. The lard can then be strained and stored in jars and will keep for years. I have seen it used [as a plaster for burns] with great success. [Ballyclough, Co. Cork, October 1990]
>
> We had to pull a big bunch of coarse ivy leaves. Chop them up and stew them until soft. Keep the juice and put in an old container. Discard the leaves. With an old clothes brush take your husband's serge suit and proceed to brush in the liquid. . . . Then take a clean cloth and iron it all over. It's like new. A lot cheaper than dry cleaning. [Castlerock, Co. Derry, February 1989][16]

The age-old belief that plants, particularly trees, possess protective and/or destructive powers lingers:

> When my brother and sister-in-law moved to a new house in south Devon . . . 30 years ago, they were told that the bay trees which grew at the entrance would protect the house, but my sister-in-law said they didn't, because she always said the house had a ghost. [Oxford, January 1991][17]

The association of plant with supranatural forces and beings is often considered superstition but is not completely ignored:

> As a child [in Yorkshire] I used to pick masses of bluebells, but my mother would never let me bring them into the house. . . . I tried to dismiss this kind of thing as superstitious nonsense, but found it most disturbing when my small son brought me a bunch of bluebells on May Day last year and insisted that we had them inside. [Stetchworth, Cambridgeshire, December 1991][18]

Such customs may continue, even when a rational basis for the belief is known:

> [In the Lake District] the belief that when blackberries have been frosted they become Devil's Fruit and are no longer fit for human consumption is still held locally. [Rowling, 1976: 101]
>
> Blackberries should not be eaten after Michaelmas Day (29 September) as they have the devil in them after that. This has much truth in it in that a fungus attacks the plants about them, I believe. Personally I don't eat them after that day because I imagine they are probably unpalatable! They are usually wet and nasty anyway. [Stoke Bishop, Avon, December 1982][19]

In keeping with the spirit of the present volume, we should turn our attention briefly to the subject of our study: the plants. Wild and cultivated flora was an integral part of medieval life at all social levels, while today gardens are a luxury or a burden for many, and herbs are seen most often in dried form, in health food stores for curative purposes, and at the grocers for culinary use. But garden historians are mining the early treatises, archaeological and documentary evidence, literature and art, and other sources to reconstruct the image of medieval gardens, and encouraging their re-creation. A number have been produced in England and elsewhere by societies, trusts, and museums at historical sites and other locations, including pleasure, kitchen, physic, and formal and informal herb gardens that honor the plants' beauty, function, and cultural significance. Individuals who wish to create their own garden can find designs, instructions, plant and material lists, and other resources in various publications. Those of us with limited or no planting space can have a windowsill herb garden, and each time we take a snip of chives or a sprig of parsley from our own "kitchen garden," we are reconnected briefly, and sweetly, with the past.

APPENDIX B

LIST OF PLANTS

Not all of the plants in Middle-earth could be discussed on our tour, and there are undoubtedly some that have been overlooked. Hopefully they will be discovered by observant travelers, who will learn their stories and add them to the list.

Flowers

Amaranth
Anemone
Asphodel
Belladonna
Briar (*Rosa canina;* dog rose; wild rose)
Camellia
Celandine
Clematis
Daisy
Daffodil
Dianthus (gillyflower; clove-pink)
Eglantine (*Rosa eglanteria;* sweet briar)
Hyacinth (bluebell)
Iris

Lily
Lobelia
Marigold
Nasturtium
Pansy (heartsease)
Peony
Pimpernel
Poppy
Primerole (*Primrose vulgaris;* primula)
Rose
Saxifrage (rockfoil)
Snapdragon
Stonecrop
Sunflower
Water lily

Herbs

Marjoram
Mentha (mint)
Mugwort

Parsley
Sage (*Salvia*)
Thyme

Shrubs/Miscellaneous

Angelica
Bramble (blackberry)
Broom
Butterbur
Cresses*
Fern (bracken)
Fireweed (willow herb)
Gorse (whin; furze)
Heather (ling)
Hemlock
Holly

Ivy
Mushroom
Nettle
Parsley, cow (wood)
Pole beans
Reeds*
Rushes*
Sloe (blackthorn)
Thistle*
Thornbush*
Whortleberry (bilberry)

Trees

Alder
Ash
Bay
Beech
Birch
Box
Cedar
Cypress
Cornel (dogwood)
Elm
Filbert
Fir
Hawthorn
Hazel

Holm-oak
Juniper
Larch
Linden
Myrtle
Oak
Olive
Pine
Rowan (mountain ash; quick-
    beam; whitty tree)
Tamarisk
Terebinth
Willow (withy)
Yew

Fictive

Athelas   Mallorn
Alfirin   Mallos
Elanor   Niphredil
Lebethron   Simbelmynë (Evermind)

*Generic plant group—no species named.

NOTES

Introduction

1. J. R. R. Tolkien, "On Fairy-stories," *The Tolkien Reader* (New York: Ballantine Books, 1966), 87.

2. J. R. R. Tolkien, *The Letters of J. R. R. Tolkien,* ed. Humphrey Carpenter (Boston: Houghton Mifflin, 1981), 402 (hereafter *Letters*).

3. *Letters,* 79, 71, 102, 107, 79, 87, 403.

4. George Sayer, "Recollections of J. R. R. Tolkien," *Mythlore* 21.2 (Winter 1996): 22.

5. Information on the plants' history, uses, and lore is a compendium derived from a number of sources, which are listed in the bibliography. In particular, see Nicholas Culpeper, *Culpeper's Complete Herbal and English Physician,* (1826; repr., Manchester, U.K.: Harvey Sales, 1981); Brent Elliott, *Flora: An Illustrated History of the Garden Flower* (Buffalo, N.Y.: Firefly Books, 2001); Geoffrey Grigson, *The Englishman's Flora* (London: J. M. Dent & Sons, 1955); Miranda Innes and Clay Perry, *Medieval Flowers* (London: Kyle Cathie, 1997); Christopher Lloyd and Richard Bird, *The Cottage Garden* (New York: DK Publishing, 1990); and Rob Talbot and Robin Whiteman, *Brother Cadfael's Herb Garden: An Illustrated Companion to Medieval Plants and Their Uses* (Boston: Little, Brown, 1997).

1. Hobbit Names

1. J. R. R. Tolkien, *The Fellowship of the Ring* (New York: Ballantine Books, 1965), bk. 1, chap. 9 (hereafter *Fellowship*).

2. Grigson, *Englishman's Flora,* 382–83.

3. See appendix A, "About Plant Lore," this volume.

4. *Letters,* 348.

5. Ibid., 407.

6. Ibid., 409.

7. Ibid., 26, 329, 88.

8. Translations from Old Norse by Patricia Terry, *Poems of the Vikings: The Elder Edda* (Indianapolis: Bobbs-Merrill, 1969), 9–11.

9. *Fellowship,* bk. 2, chap. 6.

10. *Letters,* 87.

11. J. R. R. Tolkien, *The Hobbit* (New York: Ballantine Books, 1966), 28 (hereafter *Hobbit*).

12. J. R. R. Tolkien, *The Return of the King* (New York: Ballantine Books, 1965), bk. 6, chap. 3 (hereafter *Return*).

13. Elliott, *Flora,* 36.

14. *Letters,* 403.

15. *Fellowship,* bk. 1, chap. 1.

16. Medieval names, identification, and description of plants' appearance do not always correspond to the modern plants, which is the study of a complex area of botanical research.

17. For a brief history of the cottage garden, see Lloyd and Bird, "The Cottage Garden Tradition," in *The Cottage Garden.*

18. Culpeper, *Culpeper's Complete Herbal,* 90.

19. Jill Duchess of Hamilton, Penny Hart, and John Simmons, *The Gardens of William Morris* (New York: Stewart, Tabori & Chang, 1999), 22.

20. Elliott, *Flora,* 74.

21. Culpeper, *Culpeper's Complete Herbal,* 71.

22. Talbot and Whiteman, *Brother Cadfael's Herb Garden,* 161.

23. Ibid., 160.

24. Penelope Hobhouse, *Penelope Hobhouse's Gardening through the Ages* (New York: Simon and Schuster, 1992), 73.

25. Elliott, *Flora,* 32.

26. Ibid., 135.

27. Roy Vickery, *Oxford Dictionary of Plant-Lore* (Oxford: Oxford Univ. Press, 1995), 221.

28. *Hobbit,* 16.

29. Culpeper, *Culpeper's Complete Herbal,* 104–5.

30. *Letters,* 295.

31. Talbot and Whiteman, *Brother Cadfael's Herb Garden,* 155.

32. Elliott, *Flora,* 265.

33. Ibid., 20.

34. Middle English quotation is from *The Poems of the Pearl Manuscript,* ed. Malcolm Andrew and Ronald Waldron (Berkeley: Univ. of California Press, 1978); translation is from *Sir Gawain and the Green Knight, Pearl, and Sir Orfeo,* trans. J. R. R. Tolkien (New York: Ballantine Books, 1975).

35. Qtd. in Kay N. Sanecki, *History of the English Herb Garden* (London: Ward Lock, 1992), 35.

36. Ruth S. Noel, *The Mythology of Middle-earth* (Boston: Houghton Mifflin, 1977), 118–20.

37. *Letters,* 293–94.

38. *Return,* bk. 6, chap. 8.

2. From Shire to Mordor

1. *Fellowship,* bk. 2, chap. 9.

2. For Tolkien's attitude toward the use of archaisms, see Letter 171 and his prefatory remarks to *Beowulf and the Finnesburg Fragment: A Translation into Modern English Prose,* trans. John R. Clark Hall (London: George Allen & Unwin, 1940), xiv-xvii.

3. *Letters,* 183.

4. Sayer, "Recollections," 23.

5. *Letters,* 161.

6. Ibid., 178.

7. Ibid., 192.

8. *Fellowship,* bk. 1, chap. 7.

9. *Letters,* 417, 420.

10. Middle English quotation is from *The Poems of the Pearl Manuscript,* ed. Malcolm Andrew and Ronald Waldron (Berkeley: Univ. of California Press, 1978); translation is Tolkien's.

11. *Fellowship,* bk. 1, chap. 3.

12. *Letters,* 402.

13. *Fellowship,* bk. 1, chap. 7.

14. *Letters,* 199–200.

15. See John Tinkler, "Old English in Rohan," in *Tolkien and the Critics: Essays on J. R. R. Tolkien's The Lord of the Rings,* ed. Neil D. Isaacs and Rose A. Zimbardo (Notre Dame: Univ. of Notre Dame Press, 1969), 164–69.

16. J. R. R. Tolkien, "A Secret Vice," *The Monsters and the Critics and Other Essays,* ed. Christopher Tolkien (London: George Allen & Unwin, 1983), 198.

17. *Letters,* 231.

18. *Fellowship,* bk. 2, chap. 2.

19. *Return,* bk. 5, chap. 5.

3. Ithilien

1. J. R. R. Tolkien, *The Two Towers* (New York: Ballantine Books, 1965), bk. 4, chap. 6; bk. 4, chap. 2 (hereafter *Two Towers*).

2. Ibid., bk. 4, chap. 2.

3. *Letters,* 79.

4. Hamilton, Hart, and Simmons, *The Gardens of William Morris,* 90.

5. *Letters,* 73.

6. Qtd. in Grigson, *The Englishman's Flora,* 129.

7. Hamilton, Hart, and Simmons, *The Gardens of William Morris,* 98.

8. Culpeper, *Culpeper's Complete Herbal,* 42.

9. Talbot and Whiteman, *Brother Cadfael's Herb Garden,* 138, 172, 184; Vickery, *Oxford Dictionary of Plant-Lore,* 328.

10. See Betsy Clebsch, *A Book of Salvias: Sages for Every Garden* (Portland, Ore.: Timber Press, 1997), for information on the many varieties of salvia.

11. *Fellowship,* bk. 1, chap. 11.

12. *Letters,* 221, 420.

13. Ibid., 417.

14. The derivation of Gladden Fields and Gladden River is the Old English word for iris, "glædene," which Tolkien supposes to refer to the yellow flag, even though the modern English "gladdon" refers to *Iris foetidissima* (Ibid., 381).

15. Culpeper, *Culpeper's Complete Herbal,* 62.

16. Vickery, *Oxford Dictionary of Plant-Lore,* 409.

17. *Letters,* 106.

18. Wayne G. Hammond and Christina Scull, *J. R. R. Tolkien: Artist and Illustrator* (Boston: Houghton Mifflin, 2000), 193.

19. *Letters,* 341.

20. Ibid., 321.

4. Forests and Trees

1. Humphrey Carpenter, *Tolkien: A Biography* (New York: Ballantine Books, 1977), 181.

2. *Letters,* 342.

3. Hammond and Scull, *J. R. R. Tolkien,* 65.

4. Tolkien, "On Fairy-stories," 56.

5. *Fellowship,* bk. 1, chap. 3.

6. J. R. R. Tolkien, "Leaf by Niggle," in *Tree and Leaf* (Boston: Houghton Mifflin, 1965), viii. In Letter 241, Tolkien tells the story of the tree's mutilation and valiant attempt at recovery, but he believes it to be standing rather than cut down as related in the introductory note to *Tree and Leaf* cited above.

7. Tolkien, "Leaf by Niggle," 95.

8. Carpenter, *Tolkien,* 24.

9. *Letters,* 419–20.

10. Ibid., 420.

11. *Poems of the Elder Edda,* trans. Patricia Terry, rev. ed. (Philadelphia: Univ. of Pennsylvania Press, 1990), 208.

12. Ibid., 97.

13. *Letters,* 217.

14. *Letters,* 185.

15. Ibid., 176. One of the traditional and folkloric aspects of elvish nature is an association with evil and grotesqueness, which Tolkien avoids. For example, the heroine of Chaucer's "The Man of Law's Tale" (with which Tolkien was undoubtedly familiar) is falsely accused of being an "elf," an evil spirit "ycomen by charmes or by sorcerie" and giving birth to a "feendly creature" (754–55, 751).

16. Stephen Pollington, *Leechcraft: Early English Charms, Plant Lore, and Healing* (Frithgarth: Anglo-Saxon Books, 2000), 459.

17. *Fellowship,* bk. 1, chap. 7.

18. However, Tolkien deplored the vision of Lórien as "a fairy-castle" with tiny, delicate minarets proposed for an animated film (*Letters,* 261, 274).

19. *Fellowship,* bk. 2, chap. 8.

20. *Letters,* 211–12n.

21. *Two Towers,* bk. 3, chap. 6.

22. *Return,* appendix F.

23. *Two Towers,* bk. 3, chap. 8.

24. Ibid., bk. 3, chap. 4.

25. *Letters,* 212.

26. *Two Towers,* bk. 3, chap. 4.

27. Qtd. in Grigson, *The Englishman's Flora,* 174.

28. Pollington, *Leechcraft,* 456; Grigson, *The Englishman's Flora,* 174–75.

29. Pollington, *Leechcraft,* 497.

30. Stephen Pollington, *Rudiments of Runelore* (Frithgarth: Anglo-Saxon Books, 1995), 50. Runes and verses are reproduced with the permission of Anglo-Saxon Books.

31. Ibid., 48.

32. Richard Schindler, "The Expectant Landscape: J. R. R. Tolkien's Illustrations for *The Hobbit,*" in *J. R. R. Tolkien: The Hobbit: Drawings, Watercolors, and Manuscripts* (Milwaukee, Wisc.: Patrick and Beatrice Haggerty Museum of Art, Marquette Univ., 1987), 24.

33. Christopher Dyer's *Everyday Life in Medieval England* (London: Hambledon and London, 2000) is particularly informative and readable, as are his other works on medieval material culture.

34. *Two Towers,* bk. 3, chap. 4.

35. Tolkien, "On Fairy-stories," 62.

36. *Return,* bk. 6, chap. 8.

37. Carpenter, *Tolkien,* 21–22; "Countryside to City: How Sarehole Became Part of Suburbia," available at http://www.birmingham.gov.uk/sarehole.bcc (accessed Aug. 29, 2003); "Sarehole Mill," Birmingham Museums & Art Gallery, available at http://www.bmag.org.uk/index (accessed Aug. 29, 2003).

38. Charles Dickens, *Hard Times* (New York: New American Library, 1961), 70.

39. Carpenter, *Tolkien,* 139.

40. William Morris, prologue to "The Wanderer," in *The Earthly Paradise,* ed. Florence S. Boos, vol. 1 (New York: Routledge, 2002).

5. Restoration and Recovery

1. *Letters,* 210.

2. *Return,* bk. 5, chap. 9.

3. Hammond and Scull, *J. R. R. Tolkien,* 45.

4. *Letters,* 217.

5. Hammond and Scull, *J. R. R. Tolkien,* 183–84.

6. Tolkien, "On Fairy-stories," 57.

Appendix A

1. See Minta Collins, *Medieval Herbals: The Illustrative Traditions* (London and Toronto: British Library and Univ. of Toronto Press, 2000) on illustrated Greek, Latin, and Arabic herbals; Pollington, *Leechcraft,* on Anglo-Saxon herbals and leechcraft lore; and Vickery, *Oxford Dictionary of Plant-Lore,* on ethnobotany and modern plant lore.

2. Collins, *Medieval Herbals,* 27.

3. Pollington, *Leechcraft,* 45.

4. Collins, *Medieval Herbals,* 27.

5. Pollington, *Leechcraft,* 72, 74.

6. Ibid., 197.

7. Ibid., 247.

8. Ibid., 71.

9. Ibid., 407.

10. Ibid., 413.

11. Collins, *Medieval Herbals,* 25.

12. Talbot and Whiteman, *Brother Cadfael's Herb Garden,* 14.

13. Sanecki, *History of the English Herb Garden,* 52.

14. Vickery, *Oxford Dictionary of Plant-Lore,* 21.

15. Ibid., xvii.

16. Ibid., 203.

17. Ibid., 28.

18. Ibid., 40–41.

19. Ibid., 45.

BIBLIOGRAPHY

Beowulf: A Dual-Language Edition. Trans. Howell D. Chickering Jr. Garden City, N.Y.: Anchor Books, 1977.

Carpenter, Humphrey. *Tolkien: A Biography.* New York: Ballantine Books, 1977.

Chaucer, Geoffrey. *The House of Fame. The Riverside Chaucer.* 3rd ed. Ed. Larry D. Benson. Boston: Houghton Mifflin, 1987.

Clebsch, Betsy. *A Book of Salvias: Sages for Every Garden.* Portland: Timber Press, 1997.

Collins, Minta. *Medieval Herbals: The Illustrative Traditions.* London and Toronto: British Library and University of Toronto Press, 2000.

"Countryside to City: How Sarehole Became Part of Suburbia." Available at http://www.birmingham.gov.uk/sarehole.bcc. Accessed Aug. 29, 2003.

Culpeper's Complete Herbal and English Physician. 1826. Reprint. Manchester, U.K.: Harvey Sales, 1981.

Dickens, Charles. *Hard Times.* New York: New American Library, 1961.

Elliott, Brent. *Flora: An Illustrated History of the Garden Flower.* Buffalo, N.Y.: Firefly Books, 2001.

Foster, Robert. *A Guide to Middle-earth.* New York: Ballantine Books, 1971.

Grigson, Geoffrey. *The Englishman's Flora.* London: J. M. Dent & Sons, 1955.

Hamilton, Duchess of (Jill), Penny Hart, and John Simmons. *The Gardens of William Morris.* New York: Stewart, Tabori & Chang, 1999.

Hammond, Wayne G., and Christina Scull. *J. R. R. Tolkien: Artist and Illustrator.* Boston: Houghton Mifflin, 2000.

Hitchmough, Wendy. *Arts and Crafts Gardens.* New York: Rizzoli, 1998.

Hobhouse, Penelope. *Penelope Hobhouse's Gardening through the Ages.* New York: Simon and Schuster, 1992.

Innes, Miranda, and Clay Perry. *Medieval Flowers.* London: Kyle Cathie, 1997.

The Kalevala. Trans. W. F. Kirby. 1907. London: Athlone Press, 1985.

Landsberg, Sylvia. *The Medieval Garden.* London: British Museum Press, n.d.

Lloyd, Christopher, and Richard Bird. *The Cottage Garden.* New York: DK Publishing, 1990.

McLean, Teresa. *Medieval English Gardens.* New York: Viking Press, 1980.

Morris, William. *The Earthly Paradise*. Vol. 1. Ed. Florence S. Boos. New York: Routledge, 2002.

Noel, Ruth S. *The Mythology of Middle-earth*. Boston: Houghton Mifflin, 1977.

Poems of the Elder Edda. Trans. Patricia Terry. Rev. ed. Philadelphia: University of Pennsylvania Press, 1990.

Poems of the Vikings: The Elder Edda. Trans. Patricia Terry. Indianapolis: Bobbs-Merrill, 1969.

The Poetic Edda. Trans. Carolyne Larrington. New York: Oxford University Press, 1996.

Pollington, Stephen. *Rudiments of Runelore*. Frithgarth: Anglo-Saxon Books, 1995.

———. *Leechcraft: Early English Charms, Plant Lore, and Healing*. Frithgarth: Anglo-Saxon Books, 2000.

Robinson, William. *The English Flower Garden*. 1933. Sagaponack, N.Y.: Sagapress, 1995.

Sanecki, Kay N. *History of the English Herb Garden*. London: Ward Lock, 1992.

"Sarehole Mill." Birmingham Museums & Art Gallery. Available at http://www.bmag.org.uk/index. Accessed Aug. 29, 2003.

Sayer, George. "Recollections of J. R. R. Tolkien." *Mythlore* 21.2 (Winter 1996): 21–25.

Schindler, Richard. "The Expectant Landscape: J. R. R. Tolkien's Illustrations for *The Hobbit*." In *J.R.R. Tolkien: The Hobbit: Drawings, Watercolors, and Manuscripts*. Milwaukee, Wisc.: Patrick and Beatrice Haggerty Museum of Art, Marquette University, 1987.

Shakespeare, William. *The Complete Works of Shakespeare*. 3rd ed. Ed. David Bevington. Glenview, Ill.: Scott, Foresman, 1980.

Sir Gawain and the Green Knight. The Poems of the Pearl Manuscript. Ed. Malcolm Andrew and Ronald Waldron. Berkeley: University of California Press, 1978.

Sir Gawain and the Green Knight, Pearl, and Sir Orfeo. Trans. J. R. R. Tolkien. New York: Ballantine Books, 1975.

"Spring." In *Medieval English Literature*. Ed. J. B. Trapp. New York: Oxford University Press, 1973.

Talbot, Rob, and Robin Whiteman. *Brother Cadfael's Herb Garden: An Illustrated Companion to Medieval Plants and Their Uses*. Boston: Little, Brown, 1997.

Thomas, Graham Stuart. *The Graham Stuart Thomas Rose Book*. Sagaponack, N.Y.: Sagapress, 1994.

Tolkien, J. R. R. *The Fellowship of the Ring*. Part I of *The Lord of the Rings*. New York: Ballantine Books, 1965.

———. *The Two Towers*. Part II of *The Lord of the Rings*. New York: Ballantine Books, 1965.

———. *The Return of the King*. Part III of *The Lord of the Rings*. New York: Ballantine Books, 1965.

————. "Leaf by Niggle." In *Tree and Leaf.* Boston: Houghton Mifflin, 1965.

————. *The Hobbit.* New York: Ballantine Books, 1966.

————. "On Fairy-stories." In *The Tolkien Reader.* New York: Ballantine Books, 1966.

————. *Pictures by J. R. R. Tolkien.* Forward and notes by Christopher Tolkien. Boston: Houghton Mifflin, 1979.

————. *The Letters of J. R. R. Tolkien.* Ed. Humphrey Carpenter. Boston: Houghton Mifflin, 1981.

————. "Ides Ælfscyne." In *The Road to Middle-earth.* T. A. Shippey. Boston: Houghton Mifflin, 1983.

————. "A Secret Vice." In *The Monsters and the Critics and Other Essays.* Ed. Christopher Tolkien. London: George Allen & Unwin, 1983.

————. *The Silmarillion.* 2nd ed. Ed. Christopher Tolkien. Boston: Houghton Mifflin, 2001.

Vickery, Roy. *Oxford Dictionary of Plant-Lore.* Oxford: Oxford University Press, 1995.

"The Wanderer." In *Medieval English Literature.* Ed. J. B. Trapp. New York: Oxford University Press, 1973.

THE ILLUSTRATORS

GLORIA LIANG was born in Chunchun, China, and now lives in the San Francisco Bay area. The teenaged artist attends high school, and her watercolors have won local competitions in her age group. Besides art, she enjoys reading, sports, and playing chess. Illustrations: *Rosa canina.*

LINDA LOGAN is retired from a thirty-five-year career in science and now enjoys painting and teaching watercolor techniques. Her scientific background has influenced her botanically styled art. Linda's work is regularly exhibited throughout Palo Alto, California. Illustrations: *Rosa eglanteria,* poppies, pansy, primula, peony, dianthus, sunflowers.

MARSHA MELLO is recognized for her detailed illustrations and prints, drawn from a wide range of natural subjects. Book projects include *The Large Macaws* (1995), *Miniature Horses* (1998), and several children's books. She has done professional illustration work for magazines, catalogs, and brochures since 1975. Her limited edition etchings, which have become widely collected, can be found in California's Monterey Bay Aquarium, the Cleveland Botanical Garden in Ohio, and several northern California galleries. Illustrations: Nasturtium border, bramble, butterbur, holly, bracken, hawthorn, English bluebells, salvia, cow parsley, wood anemone, asphodel, yellow iris, crack willow, poplar, beeches, rowan, oak, English garden scene.

LINDA WADE was born in San Francisco and raised in the heart of the Silicon Valley in Sunnyvale, California. Growing up in the area's rich farmland, she drew orchards, birds, and various wildlife. Linda has taught children's art classes on the Stanford University campus. Her art, ranging from paintings, ink drawings, and mono prints to specialty handmade books, is sold privately and in galleries. Illustrations: Thyme.

INDEX